RICHARD ANUSZKIEWICZ

LEE BONTECOU

CHRYSSA

SALLY HAZELET DRUMMOND

EDWARD HIGGINS

ROBERT INDIANA

GABRIEL KOHN

MICHAEL LEKAKIS

RICHARD LINDNER

MARISOL

CLAES THURE OLDENBURG

AD REINHARDT

JAMES ROSENQUIST

JASON SELEY

DAVID SIMPSON

distributed by Doubleday & Company, Inc., Garden City, New York

americans 1963

edited by DOROTHY C. MILLER *with statements by the artists and others*

THE MUSEUM OF MODERN ART, NEW YORK

© The Museum of Modern Art, 1963
11 West 53 Street, New York 19, New York

Library of Congress Card Number 63-17994

Book design by Mary Ahern
Cover design by Susan Draper

Printed in the U. S. A. by Pictorial Offset Corporation

Americans 1963 is another in a series of American group exhibitions of a special type which have been held at the Museum of Modern Art at intervals ever since its founding in 1929. The first of these exhibitions, *Paintings by Nineteen Living Americans,* 1929-30, established the pattern — a small number of artists, a sizable body of work by each — which has been followed in most of the Museum's American group shows since, with the exception of historical surveys such as *American Painting and Sculpture 1862-1932, Romantic Painting in America,* 1943, and *Abstract Painting and Sculpture in America,* 1951. The immediate predecessors of the present exhibition were *Sixteen Americans,* 1959-60, *Twelve Americans,* 1956, *Fifteen Americans,* 1952, *Fourteen Americans,* 1946, *American Realists and Magic Realists,* 1943, and *Americans 1942: Eighteen Artists from Nine States.*

This year, in *Americans 1963,* the work of fifteen artists is presented. For the first time the show is equally divided between painting and sculpture. As on preceding occasions strongly contrasting personalities and points of view have been brought together. The exhibition is not designed to illustrate a trend, make classifications or favor any age group. The artists have been selected simply as individuals — fifteen painters and sculptors of such consequence that they should, I believe, be more fully known to the Museum's public. Each has had at least one showing in New York galleries, but through this exhibition many thousands of museum visitors will see their work for the first time.

* * *

On behalf of the Trustees of the Museum of Modern Art I wish first of all to thank the artists for their participation in the exhibition. I am deeply indebted to the lenders who have made so many key works of art available. For their contributions to the catalog I am grateful to the artists and to David Hayes, Katharine Kuh, Alfonso Ossorio, William Rubin and T. Henry Smith. Statements were written in 1963 for this catalog unless otherwise noted; the editors of *Art International, Art News* and *Pax* have permitted quotations from Ad Reinhardt's articles published in their pages. T. Henry Smith reserves all rights to publication of his poem about Robert Indiana. For special assistance with loans I am grateful to Richard Hirsch, Thomas M. Messer and Gordon M. Smith. I am indebted to the following for photographs of the artists: F. W. Drummond, Hollis Frampton, Evelyn Hofer, Paula Horn, H. Landshoff, Marvin P. Lazarus, Hans Namuth, O. E. Nelson, Giulia Niccolai, Irwin Charles Rapport, John Rawlings, Dick Weldon and Hall Winslow. Works of art illustrated were photographed by Oliver Baker Associates, Rudolph Burckhardt, Robert McElroy, Peter Moore, O. E. Nelson, R. Peter Petersen, Eric Pollitzer, Walter Rosenblum, Walter Russell, John D. Schiff, F. Wilbur Seiders, Soichi Sunami and Charles Uht.

Dorothy C. Miller
DIRECTOR OF THE EXHIBITION

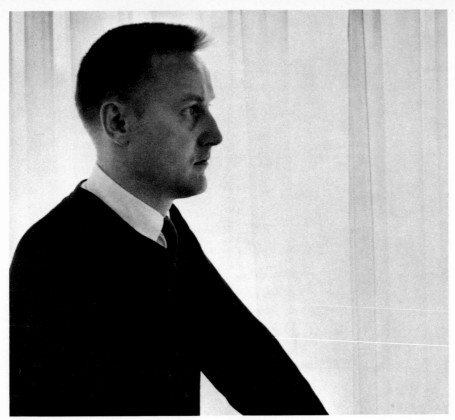

PHOTOGRAPH O. E. NELSON

Richard Anuszkiewicz

My work is of an experimental nature and has centered on an investigation into the effects of complementary colors of full intensity when juxtaposed and the optical changes that occur as a result. Also, a study of the dynamic effect of the whole under changing conditions of light, and the effect of light on color.

Richard Anuszkiewicz

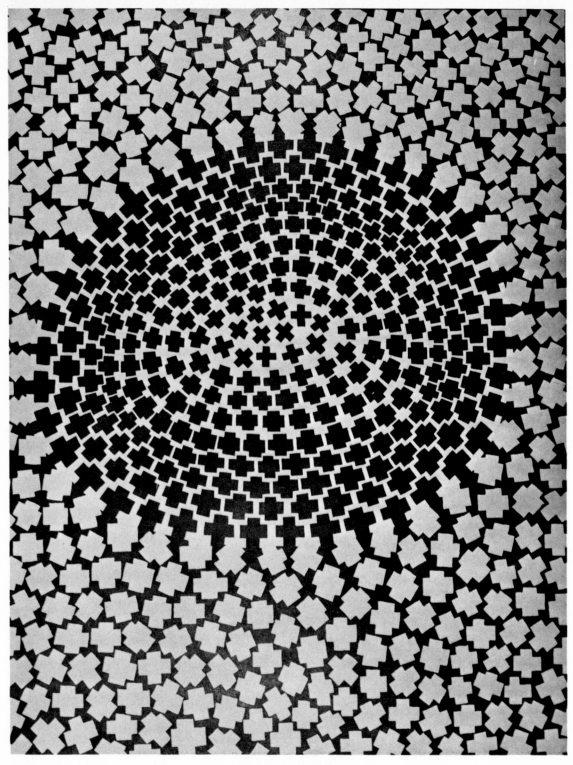

Richard Anuszkiewicz: *Plus Reversed*. 1960. Oil, 6'2½"x58¼". The James A. Michener Foundation Collection, Allentown Art Museum.

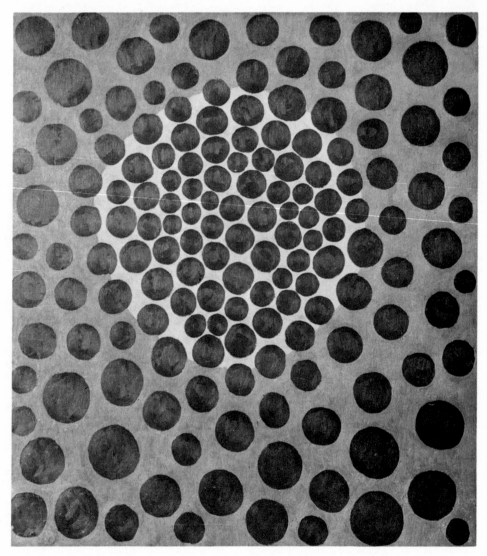

Richard Anuszkiewicz: *Fluorescent Complement*. 1960. Oil, 36x32¼″. The Museum of
Modern Art, Larry Aldrich Foundation Fund.

Richard Anuszkiewicz: *Knowledge and Disappearance*. 1961. Oil, 50x49″. Collection Warren D. Benedek.

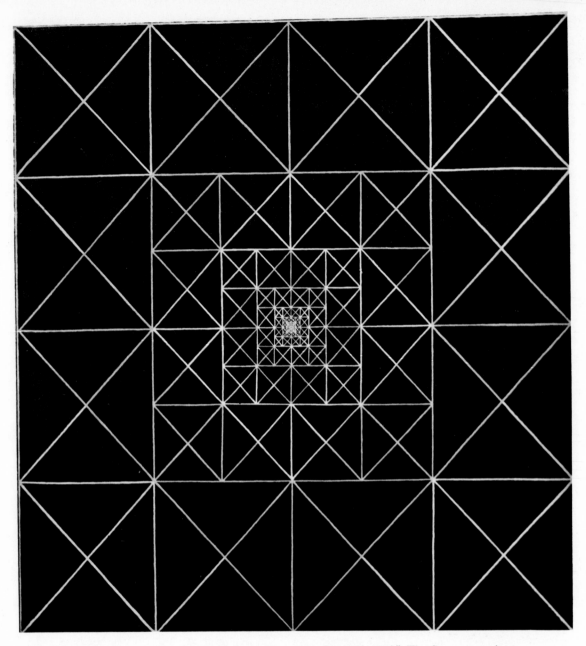

Richard Anuszkiewicz: *The Burning Glass*. 1961. Oil, 54¼x50⅛″. The Contemporaries.

Richard Anuszkiewicz: *Union of the Four*. 1961. Oil, 52¼x50″. The Contemporaries.

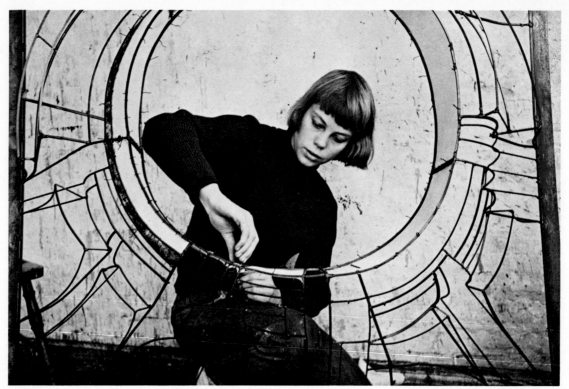

Lee Bontecou

I'm afraid I am rather vague about expressing philosophies of art and especially about my own work. I can only say that I do not know if what I am doing is art nor do I have any real concern. I just want to do what I believe and what I want to do, and what I must do to get what I want—something that is natural and something that exists in us all.

My concern is to build things that express our relation to this country—to other countries—to this world—to other worlds—in terms of myself.

To glimpse some of the fear, hope, ugliness, beauty and mystery that exists in us all and which hangs over all the young people today.

The individual is welcome to see and feel in them what he wishes in terms of himself.

Lee Bontecou
from a letter of 1960

Lee Bontecou: *Untitled*. 1959. Welded steel, canvas, wire, 58⅛x58½″. The Museum of Modern Art, gift of Mr. and Mrs. Arnold H. Maremont.

Lee Bontecou: *Untitled*. 1960-61. Welded steel, canvas, wire, 43½x50″. Albright-Knox Art Gallery

ABOVE: Lee Bontecou: *Untitled*. 1960. Welded steel, canvas, wire, 38½x31″. Collection Mr. and Mrs. Albert A. List.

LEFT: Lee Bontecou: *Untitled*. 1960. Welded steel, canvas, wire, 23x24″. Private collection.

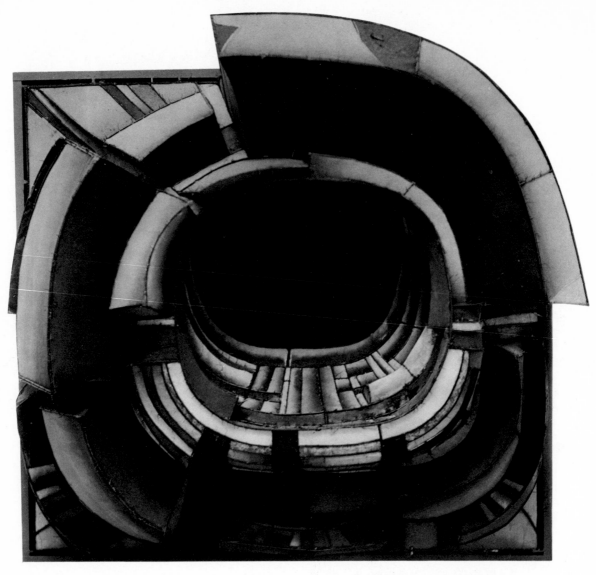

Lee Bontecou: *Untitled*. 1961. Welded steel, canvas, wire, 72x84″. Leo Castelli Gallery.

Lee Bontecou: *Untitled*. 1962. Welded steel, canvas, wire, 75x83″. Leo Castelli Gallery.

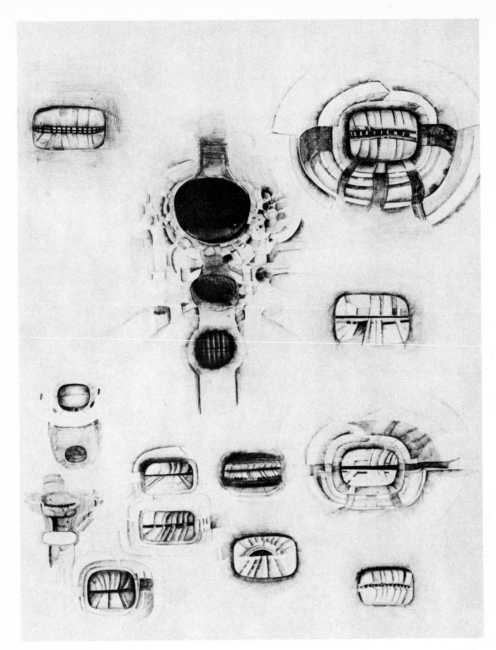

Lee Bontecou: *Drawing*. 1962. Pencil, 28½"x22½". Collection Mr. and Mrs. Robert C. Scull.

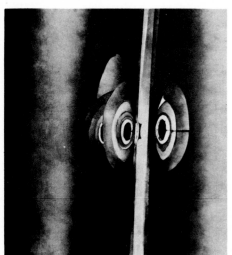

ABOVE: Lee Bontecou: *Drawing*. 1963. Pencil and soot on muslin, 36x42″.
Private collection.

LEFT: Lee Bontecou: *Drawing*. 1963. Pencil and soot on muslin, 24x18″.
Leo Castelli Gallery.

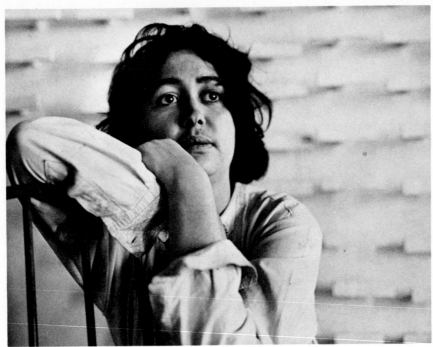

PHOTOGRAPH H. LANDSHOFF

Chryssa

Signs and symbols of communication are the subject matter of Chryssa's art: letters of the alphabet, books, newspapers, memorial tablets and directional and advertising signs. She transforms these into objects of contemplation, endowing them with the clarity of classical art. Her inspiration is contemporary and American: The New York Times and Times Square. She reveals unchanging qualities in daily phenomena and probes the essential nature of visual communication.

Her latest work, *Americanoom,* greatly surpasses in the richness and depth of its multiple aspects the individual and exacting analyses of light, space and proportion of her previous painting and sculpture. It represents a major development and synthesis in the steady evolution of her creativity.

David Hayes

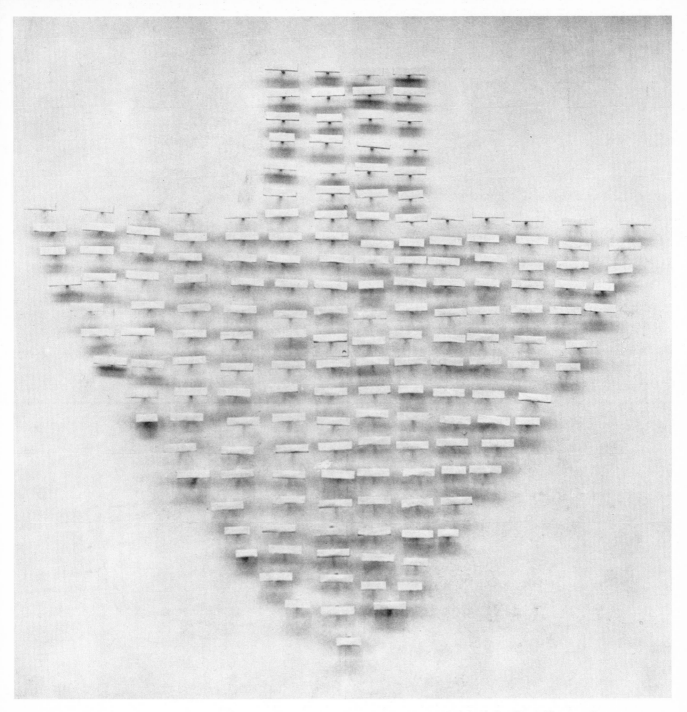

Chryssa: *Arrow: Homage to Times Square*. 1957-60. Painted aluminum relief, 8x8′. Cordier & Ekstrom, Inc.

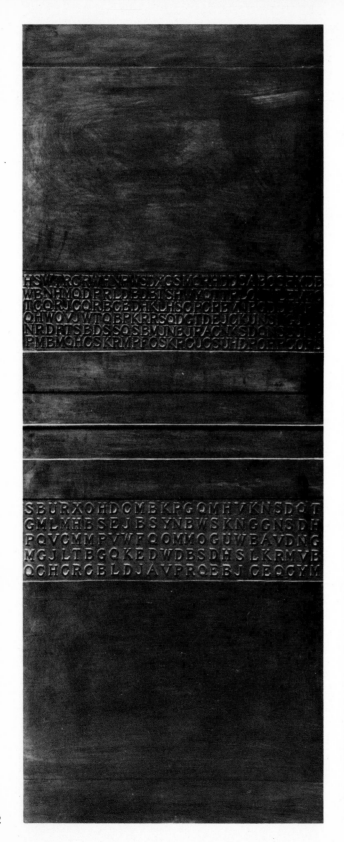

LEFT: Chryssa: *Bronze Tablet I: Homage to the Seagram Building*. 1956-59. Bronze, 57⅜x22½″. Cordier & Ekstrom, Inc.

BELOW: Chryssa: *Bronze Tablet II*. 1956-59. Bronze, 29¾x 14⅞″. Cordier & Ekstrom, Inc.

OPPOSITE: Chryssa: *Projection Letter F*. 1958-60. Welded and cast aluminum relief, 68⅜x46⅛″. The Museum of Modern Art, gift of Joseph H. Konigsberg.

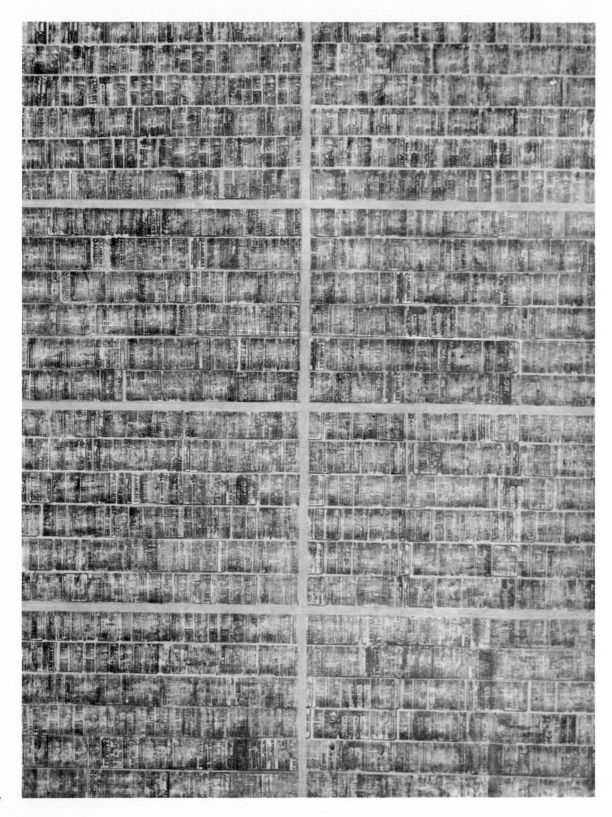

24

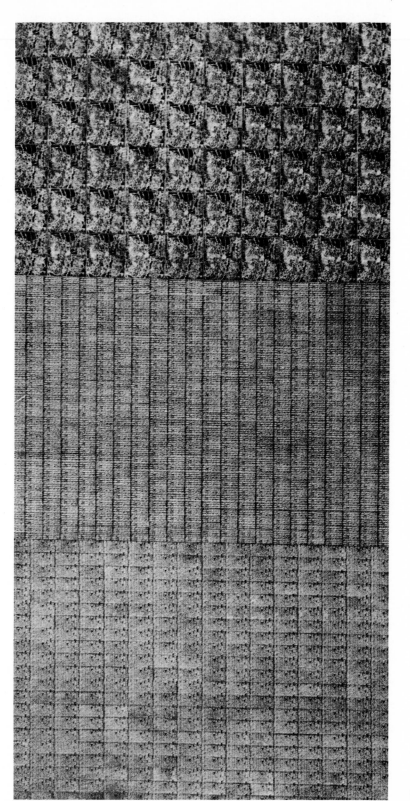

ABOVE: Chryssa: *Newspaper II*. 1961. Oil, 70⅜x91⅜". Collection Philip C. Johnson.

BELOW: Chryssa: *Magic Carpet*. 1962. Oil, 6'x10'9". Cordier & Ekstrom, Inc.

Sally Hazelet Drummond

Essentially I believe that all great art is an attempt to reveal the structured, infinite and beautiful order that lies deep within all existence. I believe it is this concern which binds together all the highest forms of art down through the ages.

My vision is of a painting that declares this sensed reality in the purest and simplest terms—the total painting as the image—silent, emphatic, radiant.

Sally Hazelet Drummond

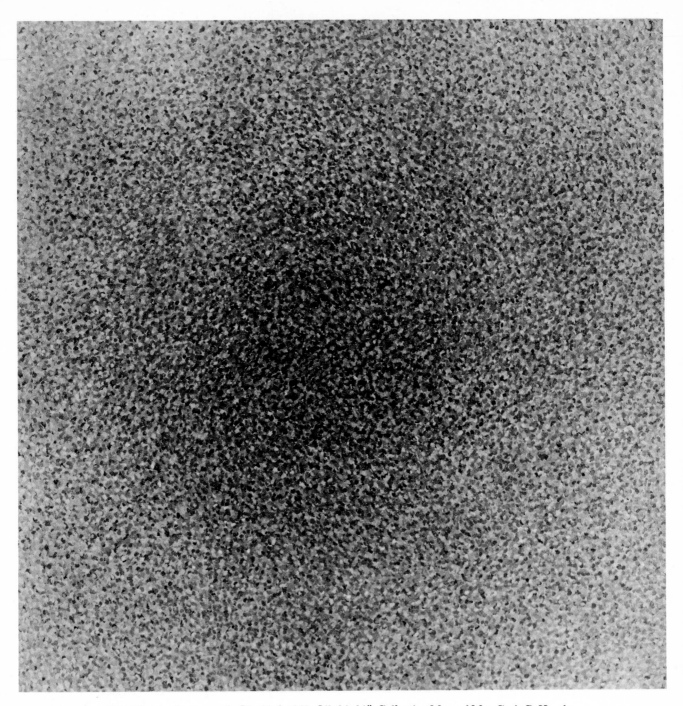

Sally Hazelet Drummond: *Bluebird*. 1960. Oil, 24x24″. Collection Mr. and Mrs. Craig P. Hazelet.

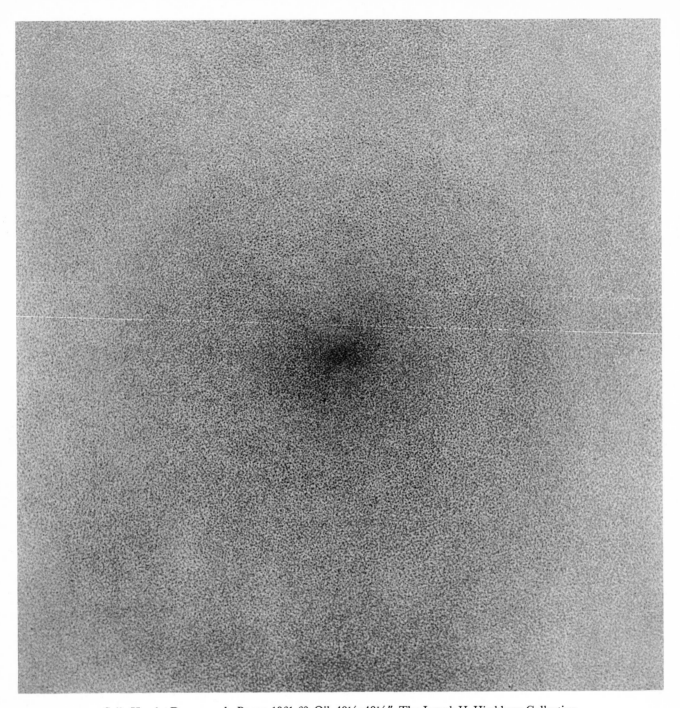

Sally Hazelet Drummond: *Drone*. 1961-62. Oil, 48¼x48¼″. The Joseph H. Hirshhorn Collection.

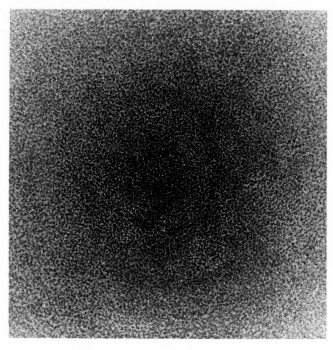

ABOVE: Sally Hazelet Drummond: *Hummingbird*. 1961. Oil, 12x12″. The Museum of Modern Art, Larry Aldrich Foundation Fund.

RIGHT: Sally Hazelet Drummond: *Pyramid*. 1961. Oil, 12x 12″. Green Gallery.

29

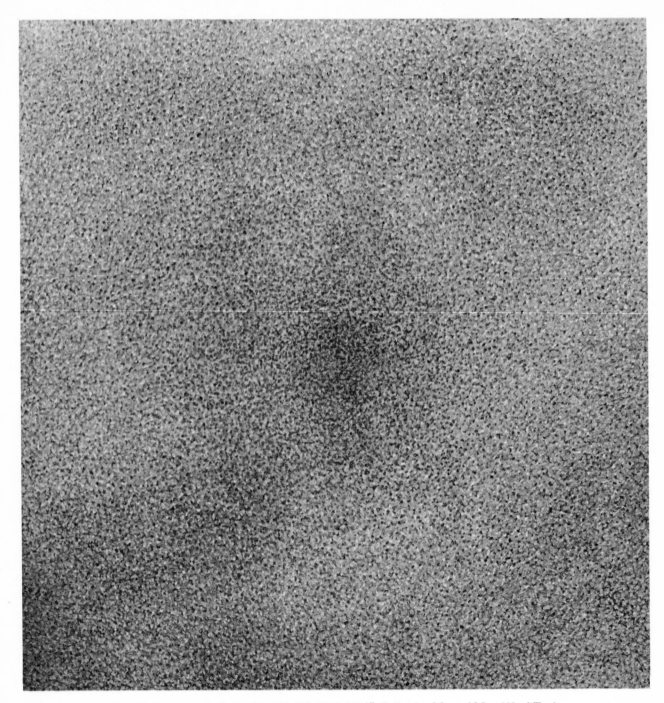

Sally Hazelet Drummond: *Fusion II*. 1960. Oil, 35¾x35¾″. Collection Mr. and Mrs. Alfred Taubman.

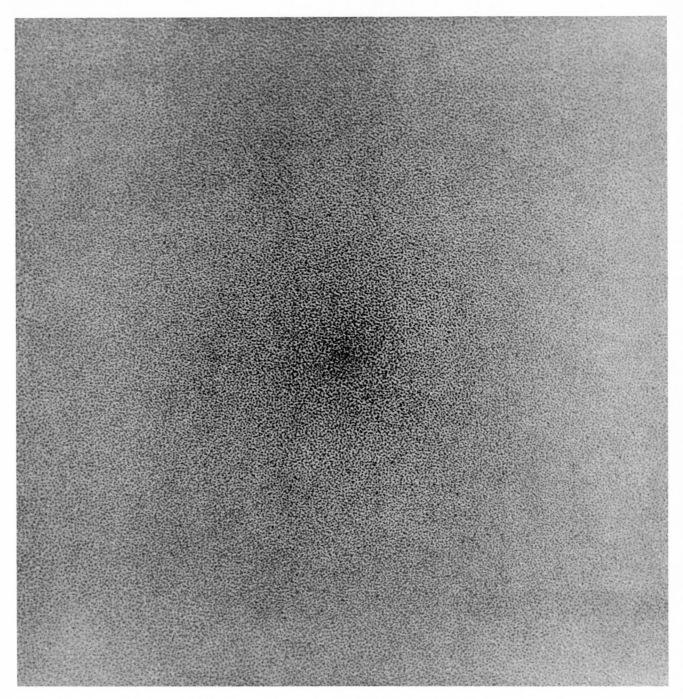

Sally Hazelet Drummond: *Target for a Golden Arrow*. 1962. Oil, 32½x32½″. Collection Mr. and Mrs. Brooks Barron.

Edward Higgins

Most of my work is based on the figure or figure groups, not as a physical display but as a basis for structural and spiritual relationships.

Competence in craft and technique frees the artist to make the broadest and most specific statement; but craft cannot be the end statement. The tinniest automobile is much better constructed than the best work of art.

Sometimes a couple of whacks with a hammer can get things going again.

As a piece of sculpture goes along it is always the next step that makes the difference—even after it is finished this can sometimes be said.

Now is the only time; things finished are no longer with me. I actually forget their physical aspects, and the things of the future won't materialize until I get to them (or there).

I haven't thought about art in years, I feel more like a witch doctor.

Edward Higgins

Edward Higgins: *Untitled*. 1960. Welded steel and plaster, 40x36″. Leo Castelli Gallery.

Edward Higgins: *Grasshopper*. 1961. Welded steel and epoxy, 24x40″. Collection Mr. and Mrs. Frederick R. Weisman.

ABOVE: Edward Higgins: *Untitled*. 1961. Welded steel and epoxy, 16x12½″. Collection I. M. Pei.

BELOW: Edward Higgins: *Double Portrait—Torsos*. 1960. Welded steel and epoxy, 16¼x17″. The Museum of Modern Art, Larry Aldrich Foundation Fund.

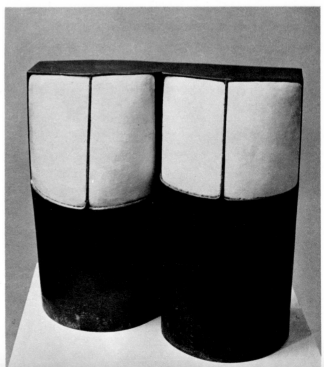

ABOVE: Edward Higgins: *Fortification*. 1960. Welded steel and epoxy, 12x15″. Private collection.

LEFT: Edward Higgins: *Pair II*. 1960. Welded steel and plaster, 27¾x16½″. Collection Mr. and Mrs. William A. M. Burden.

OPPOSITE: Edward Higgins: *Untitled*. 1963. Welded steel and epoxy, 58x30″. Leo Castelli Gallery.

Robert Indiana

there have been many american
SIGN
painters

Riding on scaffolds some and they have left their letteR
On a wall seven stories tall sometimes often they were O
Beying the monumental scale and billboards have arisen B
Eside our broad highways that are red and white and bluE
R than outdoors and we could not possibly be any happieR
That in this country every man can read eat gas and resT

In the meantime there have been some who have not been I
Nterested in billboards very much they have been more iN
Deed much more interested in us and as we have been reaD
Ing billboards they have been watching us so robert indI
Ana has been watching us we have been very interesting A
Nd we have made him interested in billboards he unfortuN
Ately now makes billboards look at us until ROBERT INDIANA

there never were any american
sign
PAINTERS

T Henry Smith
1961

38

Robert Indiana: *The American Dream #1*. 1961. Oil, 72⅛x60⅛". The Museum of Modern Art, Larry Aldrich Foundation Fund.

Robert Indiana: *God Is a Lily of the Valley.* 1961. Oil, 60x48″. Collection Mrs. Eleanor Ward.

LEFT: Robert Indiana: *Star*. 1960. Assemblage, 6'4" high. Albright-Knox Art Gallery.

RIGHT: Robert Indiana: *Moon*. 1960. Assemblage, 6'6" high. The Museum of Modern Art, Philip C. Johnson Fund.   41

Robert Indiana: *Highball on the Redball Manifest*. 1963. Oil, 60x50".
James A. Michener Foundation Collection, Allentown Art Museum.

Robert Indiana: *The Black Diamond American Dream #2*. 1962. Oil, 7'1"x7'1". Collection Mr. and Mrs. William A. M. Burden.

Robert Indiana: *The X-5*. 1963. Oil, 8'6"x8'6". Stable Gallery.

Robert Indiana: *The Demuth American Dream #5*. 1963. Oil, 12x12′. Stable Gallery.

Gabriel Kohn

Gabriel Kohn's is the first sculpture in wood to break with the tradition of the monolith. He manipulates rather than carves, but the resultant open character of his compositions owes little to Constructivism or three-dimensional collage. Where the metal sculptors who broke with the monolith emphasize linear and planar devices, Kohn insists upon the gravity of large masses. This language is his own; once seen it is easily recognized and never confused with that of other sculptors. His treatment of the material is as personal as are his forms. The sawn and laminated wood slats, glued and doweled together, recall the carpentry of the boatwright, and the marine ambiance suggested by some of his pieces (containing shapes reminiscent of rudders, prows, lobster pots and buoys) sustains this.

Kohn exaggerates when he insists that his special handling of the medium is of no importance. Yet he is right insofar as the importance of handling is clearly secondary. Kohn is not concerned with craftsmanship and his carpentry is no better than it has to be. The sculptures stand or fall by virtue of the originality of their conception—the relating of expressive shapes invented prior to, and independently of, their material realization.

A good deal of advanced modern sculpture—indeed, some of the best of it—involves the transposition of pictorial ideas into three dimensions. Kohn's work is more purely and more insistently sculptural than that. He has a central role in the revival that art is now experiencing.

Gabriel Kohn: *Chelsea Reach*. 1961. Laminated wood, 24x52″. The Museum of Modern Art, given anonymously.

ABOVE: Gabriel Kohn: *Dunkirk*. 1960. Laminated wood, 22½x44″. Collection Professor William Rubin.

OPPOSITE: Gabriel Kohn: *Tilted Construction*. 1959. Laminated wood, 27⅛x18½″. The Museum of Modern Art, Philip C. Johnson Fund.

49

BELOW: Gabriel Kohn: *Coventry*. 1962. Laminated wood, 32x40″. Otto Gerson Gallery.

OPPOSITE: Gabriel Kohn: *Acrotere*. 1960. Laminated wood, 37x39″. Otto Gerson Gallery.

PHOTOGRAPH HANS NAMUTH

Michael Lekakis

The distillation to which Michael Lekakis subjects his concepts results in a surface simplicity, a compression of energy, that at first glance belies the fecundity of his work. Used to the clang and effervescence of "Pop Art," the odor of "do-it-yourself" rising from much work in plastics and alloys, and the flaccid optical shocks we meet today, it requires an almost conscious effort to meet the artist at a level where the force and depth of his message can be felt.

He carves directly in wood; his titles are allusively classical; his forms are essentially biomorphic: yet the resulting works emanate a timeless evocativeness all the more contemporary for its traditional roots. The material is pushed to extremes of tension unforeseen in wood—the continuous springing, floating and return of *Chorós;* the illuminating uncoiling of *Python,* that is both serpent and possessing spirit. There is a continual inter-evocation between form and title. The funneling hollow within *Choani* is repeated positively in the uncoiling spirals that it supports; its rhythms move from abyss, to growing solid, to the void without. This same coiled dynamic force sustains *Helix* (it is interesting to compare the formal similarity of this small sculpture to the Helicoide de la Roca Tarpeya in Caracas). The pulsations of *Palmos I* in which the rhythmic growth compresses itself and ceases when turned towards the pull of gravity, the unburgeoned potential inherent in *Kyesis,* the sense of atmospheric flight in *Ptisis* and the movement of further release in *Anapteroma* are clear examples of Lekakis' fulfillment of "how to do more than express oneself." Finally, the contrast between the groping vertical forms of *Aititos* and the implicitly unending prayer of *Ikesia* are superb visualizations of Teilhard de Chardin's "Man, the axis and the 'arrow' of evolution."

As Lekakis has fertilized both traditional materials and concepts to produce works that are witnesses to the involving non-absurdity of existence, so too he links Heraclitus' "informing rhythm of events and order in change" with a newly clarified and united vision of reality.

Alfonso Ossorio

ABOVE: Michael Lekakis: *Kyesis*. 1947-58. Walnut, 15″ high. Howard Wise Gallery.

LEFT: Michael Lekakis: *Helix*. 1957-63. Elm, 16″ high. Howard Wise Gallery.

Michael Lekakis: *Anapteroma*. 1955-58. Ash, 42″ high.
Collection Mr. and Mrs. Howard Wise.

Michael Lekakis: *Python*. 1947-60. Cherry, 39″ high. Howard Wise Gallery.

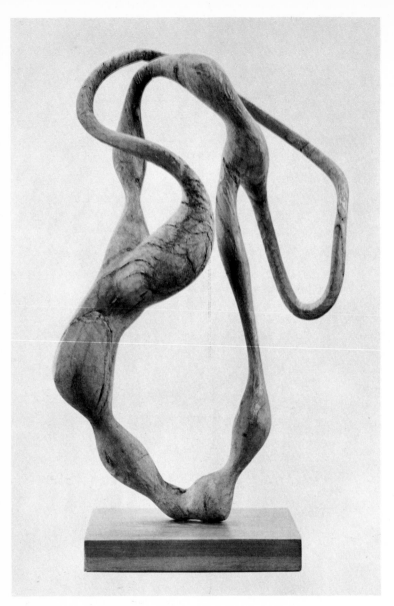

Michael Lekakis: *Dance* (*Choros*). 1954-58. Sassafras, 30″ high. Solomon R. Guggenheim Museum.

Michael Lekakis: *Ptisis.* 1957-62. Oak, 35″ high. The Museum of Modern Art, gift of the artist under the Ford Foundation Purchase Program.

LEFT: Michael Lekakis: *Palmos I.* 1950-56. Cherry, 49″ high. Howard Wise Gallery.

OPPOSITE LEFT: Michael Lekakis: *Choani.* 1956-59. Oak, 14″ high. Howard Wise Gallery.

OPPOSITE RIGHT: Michael Lekakis: *Ikesia.* 1959-61. Cocobolo, 32″ high, on rosewood base 33″ high. Howard Wise Gallery.

PHOTOGRAPH EVELYN HOFER

Richard Lindner

I can not talk about painting.
I have now even doubts that there is such a thing as art in general.
More and more I believe in the secret behavior of human beings.
Maybe all of us are creative if we listen to the secret of our inner voice.
It should not matter in what medium we try to express this.
I think of the child and the insane.
To search and to follow that inner silence is to live a life of the highest order.
Is this art?

Richard Lindner

Richard Lindner: *The Meeting.* 1953. Oil, 60x72". The Museum of Modern Art, given anonymously.

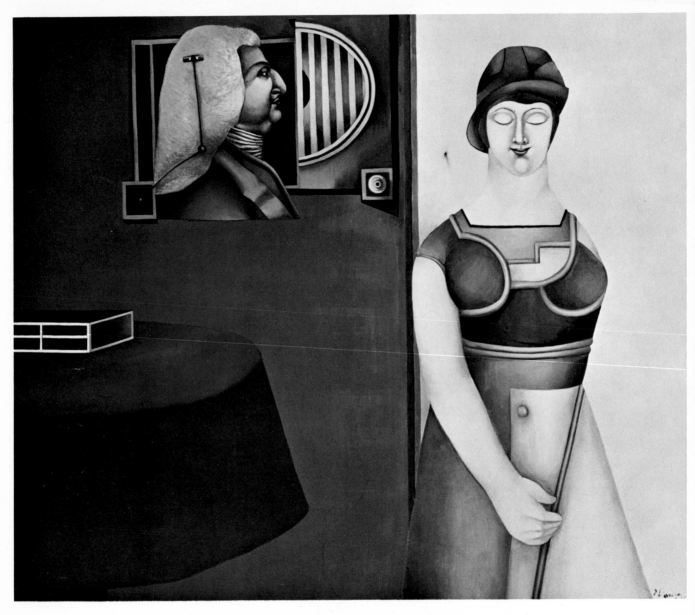

Richard Lindner: *Couple*. 1955. Oil, 50x59¾". Collection Dominique and John de Menil.

ABOVE: Richard Lindner: *Boy*. 1955. Oil, 38x26″.
Cordier & Ekstrom, Inc.

LEFT: Richard Lindner: *The Mirror*. 1958. Oil, 39⅜x
25⅝″. The Museum of Modern Art, given in memory
of Dr. Hermann Vollmer.

Richard Lindner: *The Secret*. 1960. Oil, 50x40″. Collection Myron Orlofsky.

Richard Lindner: *Napoleon Still Life*. 1962. Oil, 49½x39½". Collection Mr. and Mrs. René Bouché.

Richard Lindner: *Untitled I*. 1962. Oil, 79x50″. Cordier & Ekstrom, Inc.

Richard Lindner: *Untitled II*. 1962. Oil, 79x50″. Cordier & Ekstrom, Inc.

PHOTOGRAPH JOHN RAWLINGS

Marisol

Delicate plaster hands, impassive wooden faces, an occasional painted area of elegance—these ingredients tell little or nothing about Marisol's work, about the pathos, irony and outrageous satire with which she invests her sculpture. Whether she designs a single figure or a large group, she invariably ends up with a biting comment on human foibles. That so young an artist has mature technical control seems less surprising than that she has something of her own to say. With fertile imagination Marisol transforms daily experiences into unexpected phenomena. No one has deflated human pomposity with greater insight.

Katharine Kuh

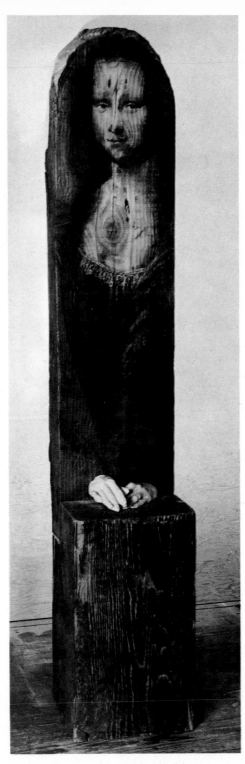

Marisol: *Mona Lisa*. 1961-62. Painted wood
and plaster, 66x11¾". Collection
Mrs. Babette Newburger.

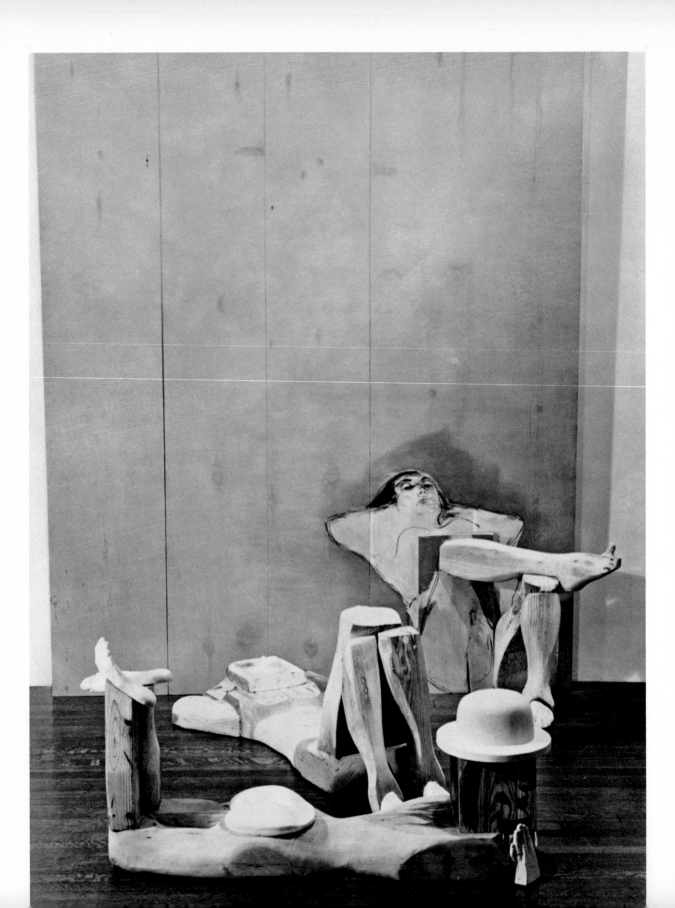

Marisol: *The Family*. 1962. Painted wood, plaster, etc., 6′10½″x65½″. The Museum of Modern Art, purchase.

OPPOSITE: Marisol: *The Bathers*. 1961-62. Painted wood, plaster, etc., 7′x70½″. Private collection.

LEFT: Marisol: *The Blacks*. 1961-62.
Painted wood, plaster, etc., 6'6"x26".
Collection Mrs. Eleanor Ward.

OPPOSITE: Marisol: *The Generals*.
1961-62. Painted wood, plaster, etc.,
7'3"x6'4". Albright-Knox Art Gallery.

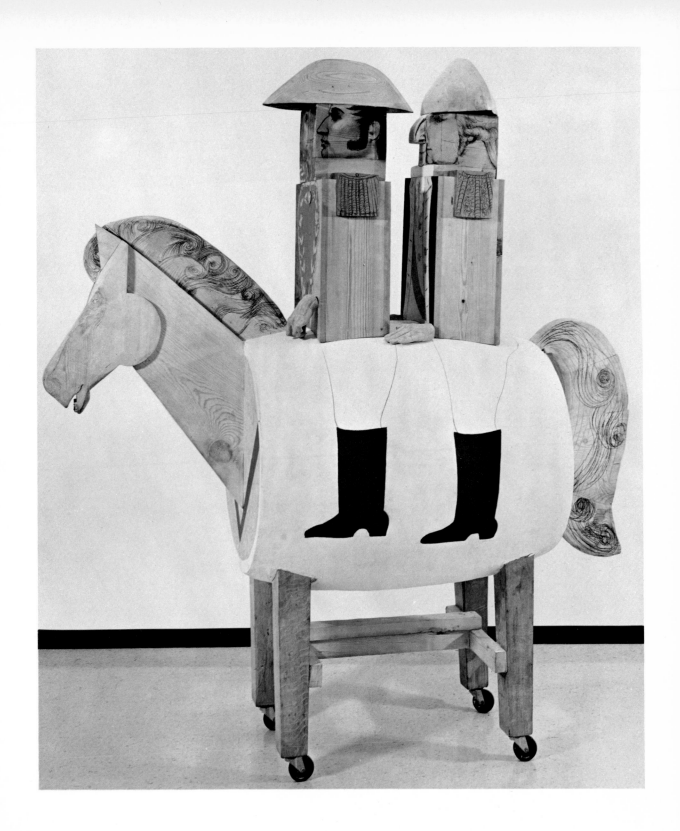

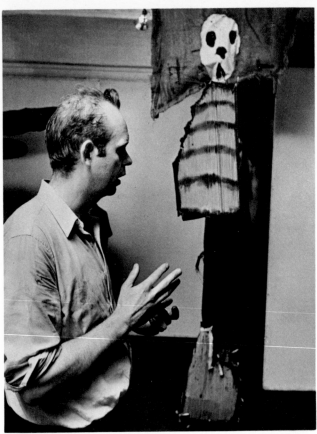

Claes Thure Oldenburg

. . . I am for an art that takes its form from the lines of life, that twists and extends impossibly and accumulates and spits and drips, and is sweet and stupid as life itself. I am for an artist who vanishes, turning up in a white cap, painting signs or hallways.

I am for art that comes out of a chimney like black hair and scatters in the sky. I am for art that spills out of an old man's purse when he is bounced off a passing fender. I am for the art out of a doggy's mouth, falling five floors from the roof. I am for the art that a kid licks, after peeling away the wrapper. I am for an art that is smoked, like a cigarette, smells, like a pair of shoes. I am for art that flaps like a flag, or helps blow noses, like a handkerchief. I am for art that is put on and taken off, like pants, which develops holes, like socks, which is eaten, like a piece of pie. . . .

I am for art you can sit on. . . . I am for art that is flipped on and off with a switch. I am for art that unfolds like a map, that you can squeeze, like your sweety's arm, or kiss, like a pet dog. Which expands and squeaks, like an accordion, which you can spill your dinner on, like an old tablecloth. I am for an art you can hammer with, stitch with, sew with, paste with, file with. I am for an art that tells you the time of day and which helps old ladies across the street.

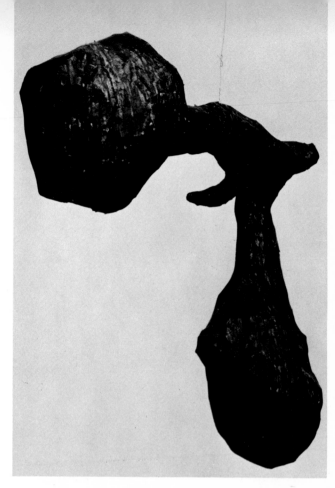

Claes Oldenburg: *Ray Gun*. 1959. Newsprint over wire frame, 39x40". Collection the artist.

I am for the art of red and white gasoline pumps and blinking biscuit signs. I am for the art of old plaster and new enamel. I am for the art of slag and black coal and dead birds. I am for the art of scratchings in the asphalt. I am for the art of bending and kicking things and breaking them and by pulling on them making them fall down. I am for the art of sat-on bananas.

I am for the art of underwear and the art of taxicabs. I am for the art of ice cream cones dropped on concrete. I am for the blinking arts, lighting up the night. I am for art falling, splashing, wiggling, jumping, going on and off. I am for the art of fat truck-tires and black eyes. I am for Kool-Art, 7-Up-Art, Pepsi Art, Sunkist Art, Dro-bomb Art, Vam Art, Pamryl Art, San-O-Med Art, 39 cents Art and 9.99 Art.

I am for the white art of refrigerators and their muscular openings and closings. . . . I am for the art of decapitated teddy-bears, exploded umbrellas, chairs with their brown bones broken, burning Xmas trees, firecracker ends, pigeon bones, and boxes with men sleeping in them. I am for the art of hung, bloody rabbits and wrinkly chickens, tambourines and plastic phonographs, and abandoned boxes tied like pharaohs.

Claes Oldenburg

from a statement for Environments Situations Spaces, *exhibition catalog, Martha Jackson Gallery, 1961*

LEFT: Claes Oldenburg: *Shirt*. 1961. Enamel paint on plaster, 48x30″. Collection Mr. and Mrs. Robert C. Scull.

BELOW: Claes Oldenburg: *Sewing Machine*. 1961. Enamel paint on plaster, 46½x63½″. Collection the artist.

OPPOSITE: Claes Oldenburg: *Red Tights*. 1961. Enamel paint on plaster, 69⅝x34¼″. The Museum of Modern Art, gift of G. David Thompson.

Claes Oldenburg: *Ice Cream Cone*. 1962. Enamel paint on plaster, 37½″ long. Collection the artist. *Not in the exhibition.*

Claes Oldenburg: *Dual Hamburgers*. 1962. Enamel paint on plaster 7x14¾″.
The Museum of Modern Art, Philip C. Johnson Fund.

Claes Oldenburg: *Strong Arm*. 1961. Enamel paint on plaster, 41x32″. Collection Mr. and Mrs. Burton Tremaine.

Claes Oldenburg: *7 Up*. 1961. Enamel paint on plaster, 54x36″. Collection Mr. and Mrs. Burton Tremaine.

PHOTOGRAPH MARVIN P. LAZARUS

Ad Reinhardt

A square (neutral, shapeless) canvas, five feet wide, five feet high, as high as a man, as wide as a man's outstretched arms (not large, not small, sizeless), trisected (no composition), one horizontal form negating one vertical form (formless, no top, no bottom, directionless), three (more or less) dark (lightless) non-contrasting (colorless) colors, brushwork brushed out to remove brushwork, a mat, flat, free-hand painted surface (glossless, textureless, non-linear, no hard edge, no soft edge) which does not reflect its surroundings — a pure, abstract, non-objective, timeless, spaceless, changeless, relationless, disinterested painting — an object that is self-conscious (no unconsciousness) ideal, transcendent, aware of no thing but Art (absolutely no anti-art). *1961*

The painting leaves the studio as a purist, abstract, non-objective object of art, returns as a record of everyday (surrealist, expressionist) experience ("chance" spots, defacements, hand-markings, accident — "happenings," scratches), and is repainted, restored into a new painting painted in the same old way (negating the negation of art), again and again, over and over again, until it is just "right" again. *1960*

A clearly defined object, independent and separate from all other objects and circumstances, in which we cannot see whatever we choose or make of it anything we want, whose meaning is not detachable or translatable, where nothing can be added and nothing can be taken away. A free, unmanipulated and unmanipulatable, useless, unmarketable, irreducible, unphotographable, unreproducible, inexplicable icon. A non-entertainment, not for art-commerce or mass-art-publics, non-expressionist, not for oneself. *1955*

Ad Reinhardt

Ad Reinhardt: *Abstract Painting, 1960-61*. Oil, 60x60″. The Museum of Modern Art, purchase.

from Art-As-Art, *Art International*, VI/10, *December 20, 1962*

The one thing to say about art is that it is one thing. Art is art-as-art and everything else is everything else. Art-as-art is nothing but art. Art is not what is not art.

The one object of fifty years of abstract art is to present art-as-art and as nothing else, to make it into the one thing it is only, separating and defining it more and more, making it purer and emptier, more absolute and more exclusive—non-objective, non-representational, non-figurative, non-imagist, non-expressionist, non-subjective. The only and one way to say what abstract art or art-as-art is, is to say what it is not.

The one subject of a hundred years of modern art is that awarenes of art of itself, of art preoccupied with its own process and means, with its own identity and distinction, art concerned with its own unique statement, art conscious of its own evolution and history and destiny, toward its own freedom, its own dignity, its own essence, its own reason, its own morality and its own conscience. Art does not need the meanings of "realism" or "naturalism," "regionalism" or "nationalism," "individualism" or "socialism" or "mysticism," or of any other ideas.

The one thing to say about art and life is that art is not life and life is not art. A "slice-of-life" art is no better or worse than a "slice-of-art" life. Fine art is not a "means of making a living" or a "way of living a life," and an artist who dedicates his life to his art, or his art to his life, burdens his art with his life and his life with his art. Art that is a matter of life and death is neither fine nor free.

The one assault on fine art is the ceaseless attempt to subserve it as a means to some other end or value. The one fight in art is not between art and non-art but between true art and false art, between pure art and action-assemblage art, between abstract art and surrealist-expressionist-anti-art, between free art and servile art. Abstract art has its own integrity, not some other "integration" with something else. Any combining, mixing, adding, diluting, exploiting, vulgarizing or popularizing abstract art deprives art of its essence and depraves the artist's artistic consciousness. Art is free, but it is not a free-for-all.

The one struggle in art is the struggle of artists against artists, of artist against artist, of the artist-as-artist within and against the artist-as-man, -animal, or -vegetable. Artists who claim that their art-work comes from nature, life, reality, earth or heaven, are subjectively and objectively rascals or rustics. The art of "figuring" or "picturing" is not a fine art. "New images of man"—figures and "nature-in-abstraction"—pictures are fakes. An artist who is lobbying as a "creature of circumstances" or log-rolling as a "victim of fate" is not a fine master-artist. No one ever forces an artist to be pure.

*   *   *

The one meaning in art comes from art-working and the more an artist works, the more there is to do. Artists come from artists, art-forms come from art-forms, painting comes from painting. The one direction in fine or abstract art today is in the painting of the same one form over and over again. The one intensity and the one perfection comes only from long and lonely routine attention and repetition. The one originality exists only where all artists work in the same tradition and master the same convention. The one freedom is realized only through the most conscious art-discipline and through the most regular studio-ritual. Only a standardized, prescribed form can be imageless, only a stereotyped image can be formless, only a formula-ized art can be formula-less. A painter who does not know what or how or where to paint is not a fine artist.

The one work for the fine artist, the one painting, is the painting of the one-size-canvas—the single-scheme, one formal device, one color-monochrome, one linear-division in each direction, one symmetry, one texture, one free-hand-brushing, one rhythm, one working everything into one dissolution and one indivisibility, each painting into one overall uniformity and non-irregularity. Everything into irreducibility, unreproducibility, imperceptibility. Nothing "usable," "manipulatable," "salable," "dealable," "collectable," "graspable." No art as a commodity or a jobbery. Art is not the spiritual side of business.

The one standard in art is oneness and fineness, rightness and purity, abstractness and evanescence. The one thing to say about art is its breathlessness, lifelessness, deathlessness, contentlessness, formlessness, spacelessness and timelessness. This is always the end of art.

from Twelve Rules for a New Academy, *Art News,* May 1957

"The Guardian of the True Tradition in Art" is the Academy of Fine Art: "to give certain rules to our art and to render it pure." The first rule and absolute standard of fine art, and painting, which is the highest and freest art, is the purity of it. The more uses, relations and "additions" a painting has, the less pure it is. The more stuff in it, the busier the work of art, the worse it is. "More is less."

The less an artist thinks in non-artistic terms and the less he exploits the easy, common skills, the more of an artist he is. "The less an artist obtrudes himself in his painting, the purer and clearer his aims." The less exposed a painting is to a chance public, the better. "Less is more."

The Six Traditions to be studied are: (1) the pure icon, (2) pure perspective, pure line and pure brushwork, (3) the pure landscape, (4) the pure portrait, (5) the pure still-life, (6) pure form, pure color and pure monochrome. "The art of painting consists of four characters: vertical and horizontal, combining and scattering." "Study ten thousand paintings and walk ten thousand miles." "Externally keep yourself away from all relationships, and internally, have no hankerings in your heart." "The pure old men of old slept without dreams and waked without anxiety."

The Six General Canons or the Six Noes to be learned are: (1) No Realism or Existentialism. "When the vulgar and commonplace dominate, the spirit subsides." (2) No Impressionism. "The artist should once and forever emancipate himself from the bondage of appearance." "The eye is a menace to clear sight." (3) No Expressionism or Surrealism. "The laying bare of oneself," autobiographically or socially, "is obscene." (4) No Fauvism, primitivism or brute art. "Art begins with the getting-rid of nature." (5) No Constructivism, craft, sculpture, plasticism, or graphic arts. No collage, paste, paper, sand or string. "Sculpture is a very mechanical exercise causing much perspiration, which mingling with grit, turns into mud." (6) No "trompe-l'oeil," interior or architectural decoration. The qualities and sensitivities of these activities lie outside free and intellectual art.

The Twelve Technical Rules (or How to Achieve the Twelve Things to Avoid) to be followed are:

1. No texture. Texture is naturalistic, mechanical, and a vulgar quality, especially pigment-texture or impasto. Palette-knifing, canvas-stabbing, paint-scumbling and other action-techniques are unintelligent and to be avoided. No accidents or automatism.

2. No brushwork or calligraphy. Hand-writing, hand-working and hand-jerking are personal and in poor taste. No signature or trade-marking. "Brushwork should be invisible." "One should never let the influence of evil demons gain control of the brush."

3. No sketching or drawing. Everything, where to begin and where to end, should be worked out in the mind beforehand. "In painting the idea should exist in the mind before the brush is taken up." No line or outline. "Madmen see outlines and therefore they draw them." A line is a figure, a "square is a face." No shading or streaking.

4. No forms. "The finest has no shape." No figure or fore- or background. No volume or mass, no cylinder, sphere or cone, or cube or boogie-woogie. No push or pull. "No shape or substance."

5. No design. "Design is everywhere."

6. No colors. "Color blinds." "Color sticks in one's eyes like something caught in one's throat." "Colors are an aspect of appearance and so only of the surface," are "a distracting embellishment," and "manifest an indiscreet personality with shameful insistence." Colors are barbaric, physical, unstable, sug-

NOTE: Sources of quotations from the ancients will be supplied by the author upon written request.

83

Ad Reinhardt: *Abstract Painting, 1960-61*. Oil, 60x60″. Betty Parsons Gallery.

gest life, "cannot be completely controlled" and "should be concealed." No white. "White is a color, and all colors." White is "not artistic, appropriate and pleasing for kitchen fixtures, and hardly the medium for expressing truth and beauty." White on white is "a transition from pigment to light" and "a screen for the projection of light" and "moving" pictures.

7. No light. No bright or direct light in or over the painting. Dim, late afternoon, non-reflecting twilight is best outside. No chiaroscuro, "the malodorant reality of craftsmen, beggars, topers with rags and wrinkles."

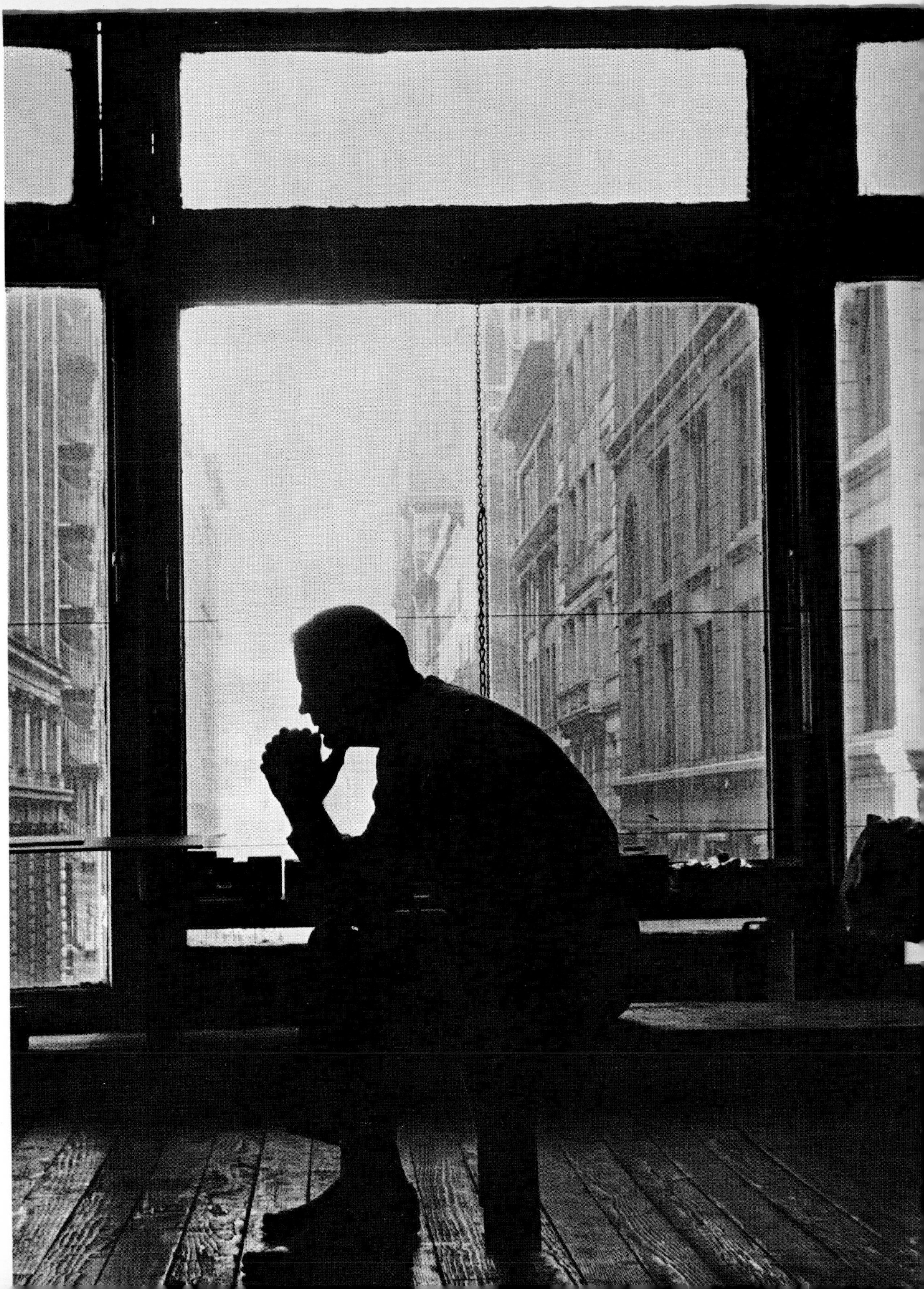

PHOTOGRAPH MARVIN P. LAZARUS

8. No space. Space should be empty, should not project, and should not be flat. "The painting should be behind the picture frame." The frame should isolate and protect the painting from its surroundings. Space divisions within the painting should not be seen.

9. No time. "Clock-time is inconsequential." "There is no ancient or modern, no past or future in art. A work of art is always present." The present is the future of the past, and the past of the future.

10. No size or scale. Breadth and depth of thought and feeling in art have no relation to physical size. Large sizes are aggressive, positivist, intemperate, venal and graceless.

11. No movement. "Everything is on the move. Art should be still."

12. No object, no subject, no matter. No symbols, images, visions or ready-mades. Neither pleasure nor pain. No mindless working or mindless non-working. No chess playing.

Supplementary regulations: No easel or palette. Low, flat, sturdy benches work well. Brushes should be new, clean, flat, even, 1 inch wide, and strong. "If the heart is upright, the brush is firm." No noise. "The brush should pass over the surface lightly and smoothly" and quietly. No rubbing or scraping. Paint should be permanent, free of impurities, mixed and stored in jars. The scent should be of "pure spirits of turpentine, unadulterated and freshly distilled." "The glue should be as clean and clear as possible." Canvas is better than silk or paper, linen better than cotton. There should be no shine in the finish. Gloss reflects and relates to the changing surroundings. "A picture is finished when all traces of the means used to bring about the end have disappeared."

The fine art studio should have a "rain-tight roof" and be 25 feet wide and 50 feet long, with extra space for storage and sink. "The room where the artist paints should be a wide and secluded chamber, warm in winter and cool in summer." Paintings should be stored away and not continually looked at. The ceiling should be 12 feet high. The studio should be separate from the home and living, "away from the claims of concubinage and matrimony."

The fine artist should have a fine mind, "free of all passion, ill-will and delusion."

*　*　*

The department of fine art should be separate from other departments in the academy-university, and its aim the education and "correction of the artist"-as-artist, not the "enlightenment of the public" or the popularization of art. The art-college should be a cloister-ivy-hall-ivory-tower-community of artists, an artists union and congress and club, a "center of consciousness and conscience," not a success-school or service-station or rest-home or house of artists' ill-fame.

*　*　*

The museum of fine art should exclude everything but fine art, and be separate from museums of ethnology, geology, archaeology, history, decorative-arts, industrial-arts, military-arts, and museums of other things. A museum is a treasure-house and tomb, not a counting-house or amusement-center. A museum should not be an art-curator's personal-monument or an art-collector-sanctifying-establishment or an art-history-manufacturing-plant or an artists' market-block.

*　*　*

The government-bureau of fine art should keep art free from free-enterprise, and when artists are unable to conduct themselves properly or are not able to govern or correct themselves, and when an art-milieu becomes over-professionalized, over-amateurized, over-irrationalized or over-managerialized, it should speak softly and carry a big stick.

Ad Reinhardt

James Rosenquist

I try to paint what I think about, while purging myself of devices that will put boundaries on my picture.

A reality may knock me on the floor and the finished picture may do the same or better, but the process in between is nerve-racking.

The manner of painting and materials used seem expendable to me just as long as they serve the idea.

The anonymity of recent history strikes me as does the time it takes to recognize things.

James Rosenquist 87

James Rosenquist: *The Light that Won't Fail, I.* 1961. Oil, 6x8'. The Joseph H. Hirshhorn Collection.

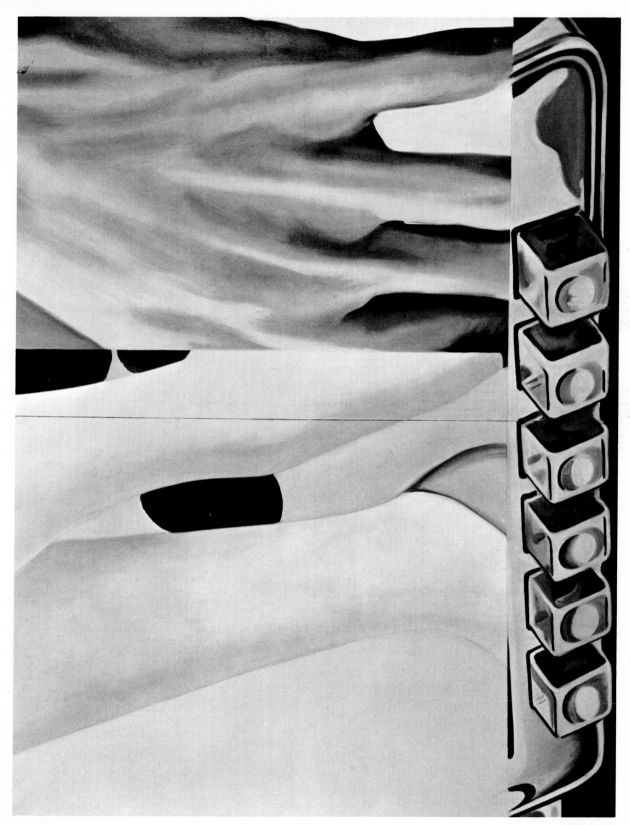

James Rosenquist: *Pushbutton*. 1960-61. Oil, 6'11"x8'9½". Collection Dott. Giuseppe Panza di Biumo.

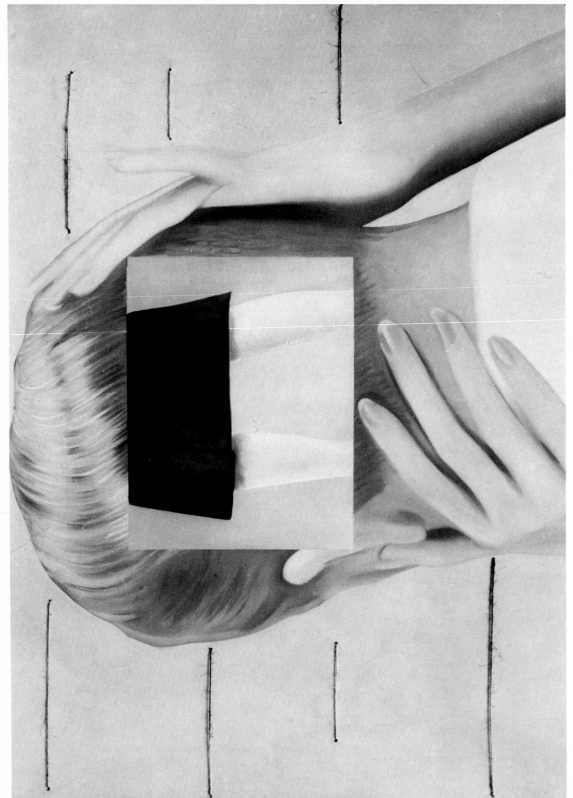

James Rosenquist: *Waves*. 1962. Oil, 56″x6′6″. Collection Dott. Giuseppe Panza di Biumo.

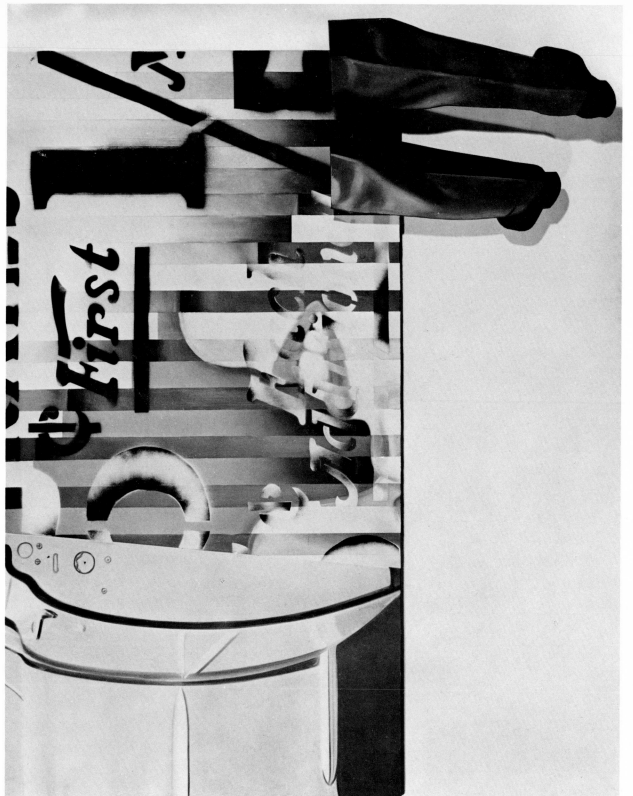

James Rosenquist: *Portrait of the Scull Family*. 1962. Oil, 6'7"x7'9". Collection Mr. and Mrs. Robert C. Scull.

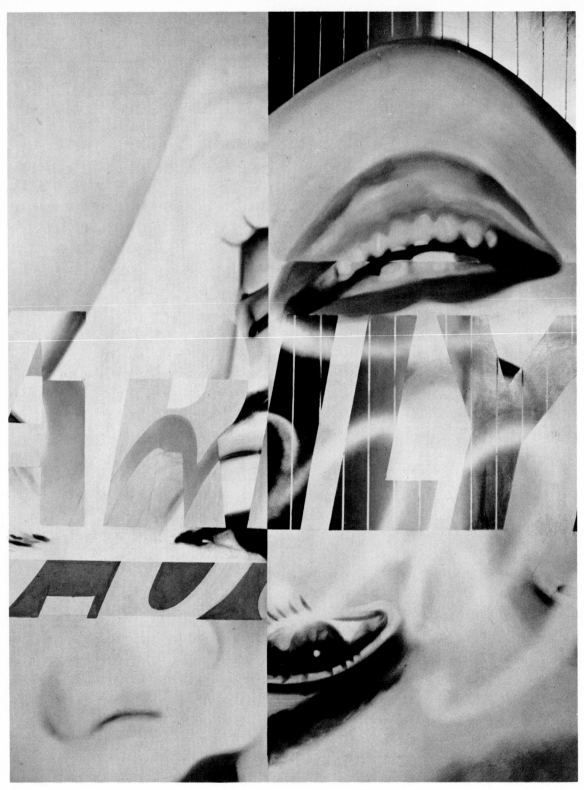

James Rosenquist: *Marilyn Monroe I*. 1962. Oil, 7'9"x6'. Collection Sidney Janis.

James Rosenquist: *Over the Square*. 1963. Oil, 7x7'. Green Gallery.

Jason Seley

I employ auto bumpers which are, to me, inspirational. I move them around. Put them together. Add. Subtract. Then if all goes well something exciting begins to happen. It is like a voyage of discovery, like going somewhere one has not been before and that is when the going is good.

Jason Seley

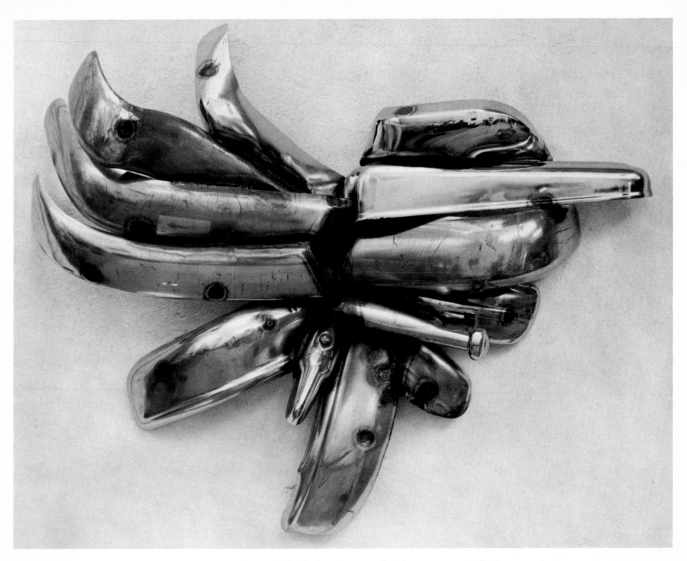

Jason Seley: *Le Roi Soleil*. 1962. Welded steel automobile bumpers, 50x63″. Kornblee Gallery.

Jason Seley: *Anjou*. 1961. Welded steel automobile bumpers, 62″ high.
Kornblee Gallery.

Jason Seley: *The Boys from Avignon*. 1962-63. Welded steel automobile bumpers, 58"x7'1". Kornblee Gallery.

Jason Seley: *The Anatomy Lesson*. 1962. Welded steel automobile bumpers, 27x53″. Kornblee Gallery.

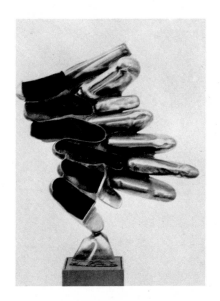

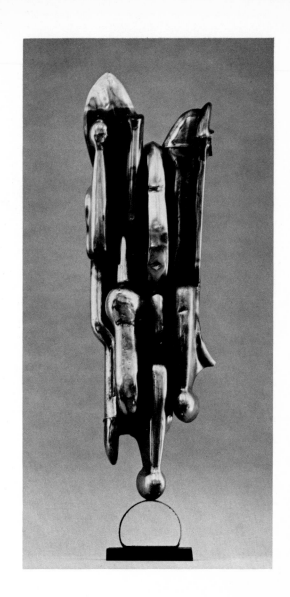

ABOVE: Jason Seley: *Canterbury*. 1962. Welded steel automobile bumpers, 46x13″. Kornblee Gallery.

LEFT: Jason Seley: *Flip*. 1963. Welded steel automobile bumpers, 30½x26″. Kornblee Gallery.

PHOTOGRAPH BILL HAWKEN

David Simpson

With painting the final criterion is how it looks. This being so, I try to make my own painting as beautiful as I can.

All theories must fall in the face of the fact of the painting, and how it looks.

During the last several years I have been interested in paintings made up primarily of horizontal stripes and bands. Some of these appear as landscape—some as "pure" painting. I've always been more interested in the painting than the landscape.

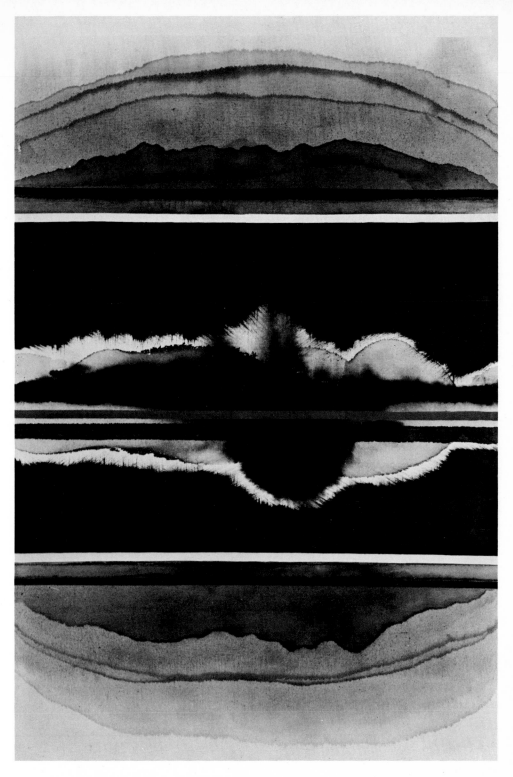

David Simpson: *Tide I*. 1961. Oil, 7'x49½". The Joseph H. Hirshhorn Collection.

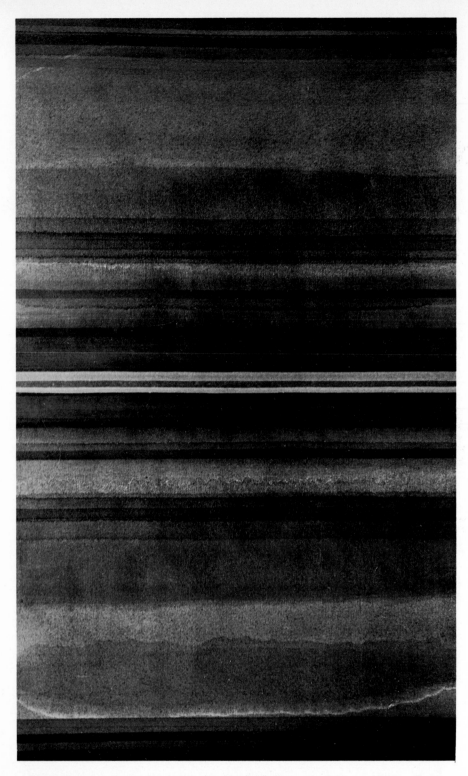

David Simpson: *Orient Line*. 1962. Oil, 60x37½". Collection Professor William Rubin.

David Simpson: *Red Blue Purple*. 1962. Oil, 48⅛″ diameter.
The Museum of Modern Art, Larry Aldrich Foundation Fund.

David Simpson: *Fire Wall*. 1962. Oil, 8′x37½″.
Robert Elkon Gallery.

David Simpson: *Earthshine*. 1962. Oil, 8′x43½″. The Abrams
Family Foundation.

BIOGRAPHIES OF THE ARTISTS AND LIST OF WORKS OF ART

An asterisk preceding the title indicates that the work is illustrated. In the dimensions, height precedes width. Lenders to the exhibition are listed on page 4.

RICHARD ANUSZKIEWICZ

Born in Erie, Pennsylvania, May 23, 1930. Studied at Cleveland Institute of Art, Cleveland, Ohio, 1948-53; Yale University, 1953-55; Kent State University, Kent, Ohio, 1955-56. Pulitzer Traveling Scholarship, National Academy of Design, 1953. Traveled in Europe and North Africa, 1958. Lives in Port Washington, New York. One-man shows: Butler Art Institute, Youngstown, Ohio, 1955; The Contemporaries, New York, 1960, 1961, 1963. In collections of Akron Art Institute, Akron, Ohio; Cleveland Museum of Art, Cleveland, Ohio; The Museum of Modern Art, New York; Butler Art Institute, Youngstown, Ohio.

Fluorescent Complement. 1960. Oil on canvas, 36x 32¼". The Museum of Modern Art, New York, Larry Aldrich Foundation Fund. Ill. p. 8.

Plus Reversed. 1960. Oil on canvas, 74⅝x58¼". The James A. Michener Foundation Collection, Allentown Art Museum, Allentown, Pennsylvania. Ill. p. 7.

The Burning Glass. 1961. Oil on canvas, 54¼x50⅛". The Contemporaries, New York. Ill. p. 10.

Union of the Four. 1961. Oil on canvas, 52¼x50". The Contemporaries, New York. Ill. p. 11.

Knowledge and Disappearance. 1961. Oil on canvas, 50x49". Warren D. Benedek, New York. Ill. p. 9.

The Harpist and the Nine Muses. 1963. Oil on canvas, 42¼x42¼". Mr. and Mrs. George D. Revington, West Lafayette, Indiana.

Moon and Sun Furnaces. 1963. Oil on masonite, 48x 48". The Contemporaries, New York.

The Symbolic City as Center of the Earth. 1963. Oil on canvas, 60x60". The Contemporaries, New York.

Wedding of the Moon and the Sun. 1963. Oil on canvas, 8x8'. The Contemporaries, New York.

LEE BONTECOU

Born in Providence, Rhode Island, January 15, 1931. Grew up chiefly in Nova Scotia. Studied at Art Students League, New York, 1952-55, with William Zorach and John Hovannes. Fulbright fellowships to Rome, 1957 and 1958; traveled in Greece and Italy.

Tiffany Foundation grant, 1959; second prize, 28th Biennial of American Art, Corcoran Gallery of Art, 1963. Lives in New York. One-man shows: Gallery G, New York, 1959; Leo Castelli, New York, 1960, 1962. In collections of Stedelijk Museum, Amsterdam, The Netherlands; Albright-Knox Art Gallery, Buffalo, New York; Museum of Fine Arts of Houston, Texas; Andrew Dickson White Museum, Cornell University, Ithaca, New York; Chase Manhattan Bank, New York; Jewish Museum, New York; The Museum of Modern Art, New York; Whitney Museum of American Art, New York; Smith College Museum of Art, Northampton, Massachusetts; Corcoran Gallery of Art, Washington, D. C.; Washington Gallery of Modern Art, Washington, D. C.

*Untitled. 1959. Welded steel, canvas and wire, 58⅛x 58½". The Museum of Modern Art, New York, gift of Mr. and Mrs. Arnold H. Maremont. Ill. p. 13.

*Untitled. 1960. Welded steel, canvas and wire, 23x 24". Private collection, New York. Ill. p. 15.

*Untitled. 1960. Welded steel, canvas and wire, 38½x 31". Mr. and Mrs. Albert A. List, New York. Ill. p. 15.

*Untitled. 1960-61. Welded steel, canvas and wire, 43½x50". Albright-Knox Art Gallery, Buffalo, New York. Ill. p. 14.

*Untitled. 1961. Welded steel, canvas and wire, 72x 84". Leo Castelli Gallery, New York. Ill. p. 16.

Untitled. 1962. Welded steel, canvas and wire, 57x 54½". Private collection, New York.

*Untitled. 1962. Welded steel, canvas and wire, 75x 83". Leo Castelli Gallery, New York. Ill. p. 17.

*Drawing. 1962. Pencil on paper, 28½x22½". Mr. and Mrs. Robert C. Scull, New York. Ill. p. 18.

Drawing. 1963. Pencil and soot on muslin, 47" diameter. Leo Castelli Gallery, New York.

*Drawing. 1963. Pencil and soot on muslin, 36x42". Private collection, New York. Ill. p. 19.

Drawing. 1963. Pencil on muslin, 47" diameter. Private collection, New York.

Drawing. 1963. Pencil and soot on muslin, 18x17". Mr. and Mrs. Leo Castelli, New York.

*Drawing. 1963. Pencil and soot on muslin, 24x18". Leo Castelli Gallery, New York. Ill. p. 19.

CHRYSSA

Born in Athens, Greece, December 30, 1933 (Chryssa Vardea Mavromichali). To Paris, 1953; studied at Académie de la Grande Chaumière. To San Francisco, 1954; studied at California School of Fine

Arts, 1954-55. To Europe, 1955; lived in Spain, Italy, England, France. Returned to United States, 1958. Lives in New York. One-man shows: Betty Parsons Gallery, New York, 1961; Solomon R. Guggenheim Museum, New York, 1961; Cordier & Ekstrom, Inc., New York, 1962. In collections of Albright-Knox Art Gallery, Buffalo, New York; Chase Manhattan Bank, New York; The Museum of Modern Art, New York; Whitney Museum of American Art, New York.

*Bronze Tablet I: Homage to the Seagram Building. 1956-59. Bronze, 57⅜x22½". Cordier & Ekstrom, Inc., New York. Ill. p. 22.

*Bronze Tablet II. 1956-59. Bronze, 29¾x14⅞". Cordier & Ekstrom, Inc., New York. Ill. p. 22.

*Arrow: Homage to Times Square. 1957-60. Painted aluminum relief, 8x8'. Cordier & Ekstrom, Inc., New York. Ill. p. 21.

*Projection Letter F. 1958-60. Welded and cast aluminum relief, 68⅜x46⅛". The Museum of Modern Art, New York, gift of Joseph H. Konigsberg. Ill. p. 23.

*Newspaper II. 1961. Oil on canvas, 70⅜x91⅜". Philip C. Johnson, New York. Ill. p. 24.

*Magic Carpet. 1962. Oil on canvas, 6'x10'9". Cordier & Ekstrom, Inc., New York. Ill. p. 25.

Americanoom. 1963. Aluminum and zinc with neon light, etc., 43"x18'. Cordier & Ekstrom, Inc., New York.

SALLY HAZELET DRUMMOND

Born in Evanston, Illinois, June 4, 1924. Attended Rollins College, Winter Park, Florida, 1942-43; Columbia University, New York, 1946-48, B.A. degree; Institute of Design, Chicago, 1949-50; University of Louisville, Kentucky, 1951-52, M.A. degree. Fulbright fellowship; in Venice, 1952-53. Lives in New York. One-man shows: Hadley Gallery, Louisville, Kentucky, 1951, 1961; Tanager Gallery, New York, 1954, 1957, 1960; Art Center Association, Louisville, Kentucky, 1957; Green Gallery, New York, 1962. In collections of The Museum of Modern Art, New York; Union Carbide Corporation, New York.

*Bluebird. 1960. Oil on canvas, 24x24". Mr. and Mrs. Craig P. Hazelet, Louisville, Kentucky. Ill. p. 27.

*Fusion II. 1960. Oil on canvas, 35¾x35¾". Mr. and Mrs. Alfred Taubman, Oak Park, Michigan. Ill. p. 30.

*Hummingbird. 1961. Oil on canvas, 12x12". The Museum of Modern Art, New York, Larry Aldrich Foundation Fund. Ill. p. 29.

*Pyramid. 1961. Oil on canvas, 12x12". The Green Gallery, New York. Ill. p. 29.

*Drone. 1961-62. Oil on canvas, 48¼x48¼″. Joseph H. Hirshhorn Collection, Greenwich, Connecticut. Ill. p. 28.

Consent. 1962. Oil on canvas, 28x28″. Joseph H. Hirshhorn Collection, Greenwich, Connecticut.

*Target for a Golden Arrow. 1962. Oil on canvas, 32½x32½″. Mr. and Mrs. Brooks Barron, Detroit, Michigan. Ill. p. 31.

EDWARD HIGGINS

Born in Gaffney, South Carolina, November 13, 1930. University of North Carolina, A.B. degree, 1954. To New York, 1956; lived and worked in Long Island City until 1962; now lives near Easton, Pennsylvania. One-man show: Leo Castelli, New York, 1960. In collections of Albright-Knox Art Gallery, Buffalo, New York; Chase Manhattan Bank, New York; The Museum of Modern Art, New York; Whitney Museum of American Art, New York.

*Double Portrait—Torsos. 1960. Welded steel and epoxy, 16¼x17″. The Museum of Modern Art, New York, Larry Aldrich Foundation Fund. Ill. p. 35.

*Fortification. 1960. Welded steel and epoxy, 12x15″. Private collection, New York. Ill. p. 36.

*Pair II. 1960. Welded steel and plaster, 27¾x16½″. Mr. and Mrs. William A. M. Burden, New York. Ill. p. 36.

*Untitled. 1960. Welded steel and plaster, 40x36″. Leo Castelli Gallery, New York. Ill. p. 33.

*Grasshopper. 1961. Welded steel and epoxy, 24x40″. Mr. and Mrs. Frederick R. Weisman, Beverly Hills, California. Ill. p. 34.

*Untitled. 1961. Welded steel and epoxy, 16x12½″. I. M. Pei, New York. Ill. p. 35.

*Untitled. 1963. Welded steel and epoxy, 58x30″. Leo Castelli Gallery, New York. Ill. p. 37.

ROBERT INDIANA

Born in New Castle, Indiana, September 13, 1928. Studied at John Herron Art Institute, Indianapolis, 1945-46; Munson-Williams-Proctor Institute, Utica, New York, 1947-1948; Art Institute of Chicago, 1949-53, where he won traveling fellowship, 1953; Skowhegan School of Painting and Sculpture, Maine, summer 1953. To Scotland; studied at University of Edinburgh and Edinburgh College of Art, 1953-54, and at University of London, 1954. Has lived in New York since 1954. Two-man show: David Anderson Gallery, New York, 1961. One-man show: Stable Gallery, New York, 1962. In collections of Albright-Knox Art Gallery, Buffalo, New York; The Museum of Modern Art, New York.

*Moon. 1960. Assemblage: wood beam with iron wheels and white paint, 6′6″ high. The Museum of Modern Art, New York, Philip C. Johnson Fund. Ill. p. 41.

*Star. 1960. Assemblage: wood beam with iron wheels and white paint. 6′4″ high. Albright-Knox Art Gallery, Buffalo, New York. Ill. p. 41.

*The American Dream #1. 1961. Oil on canvas, 72⅛ x60⅛″. The Museum of Modern Art, New York, Larry Aldrich Foundation Fund. Ill. p. 39.

*God is a Lily of the Valley. 1961. Oil on canvas, 60x 48″. Mrs. Eleanor Ward, New York. Ill. p. 40.

*The Black Diamond American Dream #2. 1962. Oil on canvas, 7′1″x7′1″. Mr. and Mrs. William A. M. Burden, New York. Ill. p. 43.

*The Demuth American Dream #5. 1963. Oil on canvas, five panels in form of a cross, 12x12′. Stable Gallery, New York. Ill. p. 45.

*Highball on the Redball Manifest. 1963. Oil on canvas, 60x50″. The James A. Michener Foundation Collection, Allentown Art Museum, Allentown, Pennsylvania. Ill. p. 42.

*The X-5. 1963. Oil on canvas, five panels assembled in X form, 8′6″x8′6″. Stable Gallery, New York. Ill. p. 44.

GABRIEL KOHN

Born in Philadelphia, June 12, 1910. Lived in Brooklyn, New York, from 1915. Studied at Cooper Union, New York, 1929, with Gaetano Cecere; Beaux Arts Institute, New York, 1930-34; assistant to Cecere, Herman MacNeil, C. P. Jennewein, Albert Stewart. Lived in New York, 1934-42, working at sculpture, also designing for theatre and films. In U. S. Army, 1942-45, with camouflage engineers. To Europe on G. I. Bill; studied with Zadkine, Paris, 1946-47. In Nice, 1947, working in terra cotta; in Rome, 1948-49; then to live in Alba, France, until 1954 except for one year at Cranbrook Academy of Art, Bloomfield Hills, Michigan, 1952-53. In New York, 1954-62. Now lives in Sarasota, Florida. One-man shows: Atelier Mannucci, Rome, 1948; Galleria dello Zodiaco, Rome, 1950; Cranbrook Academy of Art, 1953; Tanager Gallery, New York, 1958; Leo Castelli, New York, 1959; Otto Gerson Gallery, New York, 1963. In collections of Cranbrook Academy of Art; Albright-Knox Art Gallery, Buffalo, New York; The Museum of Modern Art, New York; Whitney Museum of American Art, New York.

*Tilted Construction. 1959. Laminated wood construction, 27⅛x18½". The Museum of Modern Art, New York, Philip C. Johnson Fund. Ill. p. 49.

*Acrotere. 1960. Laminated wood construction, 37x39". Otto Gerson Gallery, New York. Ill. p. 51.

*Dunkirk. 1960. Laminated wood construction, 22½x44". Professor William Rubin. Ill. p. 48.

*Chelsea Reach. 1961. Laminated wood construction, 24x52". The Museum of Modern Art, New York, given anonymously. Ill. p. 47.

*Coventry. 1962. Laminated wood construction, 32x40". Otto Gerson Gallery, New York. Ill. p. 50.

MICHAEL LEKAKIS

Born in New York, March 1, 1907, of Greek parentage. Self-taught. In U. S. Army Air Corps, 1942-45; built camouflage installations and training aids. Traveled in Mexico and Yucatan, 1945; Europe, Egypt, Greece, 1952. Lives in New York and Southampton, New York. One-man shows: Artists' Gallery, New York, 1941; Witte Memorial Museum, San Antonio, Texas, 1946; Bertha Schaefer Gallery, New York, 1946, 1948; Watkins Gallery, American University, Washington, D. C., 1949; Signa Gallery, East Hampton, New York, 1959; Howard Wise Gallery, New York, 1961. In collections of Dayton Art Institute, Dayton, Ohio; Wadsworth Atheneum, Hartford, Connecticut; Solomon R. Guggenheim Museum, The Museum of Modern Art and Whitney Museum of American Art, New York; Portland Art Museum, Portland, Oregon; Tel-Aviv Museum, Tel-Aviv, Israel.

*Kyesis. 1947-58. Walnut, 15" high, on mahogany base 15" high. Howard Wise Gallery, New York. Ill. p. 53.

*Palmos I. 1950-56. Cherry, 49" high, on mahogany base 21" high. Howard Wise Gallery, New York. Ill. p. 58.

*Dance (Choròs). 1954-58. Sassafras, 30" high. Solomon R. Guggenheim Museum, New York. Ill. p. 56.

*Anapteroma. 1955-58. Ash, 42" high, on mahogany base 31" high. Mr. and Mrs. Howard Wise, New York. Ill. p. 54.

*Choani. 1956-59. Oak, 14" high, on elm base 16" high. Howard Wise Gallery, New York. Ill. p. 59.

*Python. 1947-60. Cherry, 39" high, on mahogany base 45" high. Howard Wise Gallery, New York. Ill. p. 55.

*Ikesia. 1959-61. Cocobolo, 32" high, on rosewood base 33" high. Howard Wise Gallery, New York. Ill. p. 59.

*Ptisis. 1957-62. Oak, 35" high, on pine base 12" high. The Museum of Modern Art, New York, gift of the artist under the Ford Foundation Purchase Program. Ill. p. 57.

*Helix. 1957-63. Elm, 16" high, on mahogany base 21" high. Howard Wise Gallery, New York. Ill. p. 53.

Aititos. 1957-63. Cherry, 60" high, on pine base 15" high. Howard Wise Gallery, New York.

RICHARD LINDNER

Born in Hamburg, Germany, 1901. To New York, 1941. Studied music and painting in Munich and Berlin. Lived in Paris, 1930, 1933-41. Traveled throughout Europe and in Mexico. William and Noma Copley Foundation fellowship, 1958. Lives in New York. One-man shows: Betty Parsons Gallery, New York, 1954, 1956, 1959; Cordier-Warren Gallery, New York, 1961. In collections of The Art Institute of Chicago; The Museum of Modern Art, New York; Whitney Museum of American Art, New York.

*The Meeting. 1953. Oil on canvas, 60x72". The Museum of Modern Art, New York, given anonymously. Ill. p. 61.

*Boy. 1955. Oil on canvas, 38x26". Cordier & Ekstrom, Inc., New York. Ill. p. 63.

*Couple. 1955. Oil on canvas, 50x59¾". Dominique and John de Menil, Houston, Texas. Ill. p. 62.

*The Mirror. 1958. Oil on canvas, 39⅜x25⅝". The Museum of Modern Art, New York, given in memory of Dr. Hermann Vollmer. Ill. p. 63.

The Scream. 1958. Oil on canvas, 60x40". Mr. and Mrs. Charles B. Benenson, New York.

*The Secret. 1960. Oil on canvas, 50x40". Myron Orlofsky, White Plains, New York. Ill. p. 64.

Construction. 1962. Plastic mask, printed paper and cloth on wood panel, 11¾x13". The Museum of Modern Art, New York, purchase.

*Napoleon Still Life. 1962. Oil on canvas, 49½x39½". Mr. and Mrs. René Bouché, New York. Ill. p. 65.

*Untitled I. 1962. Oil on canvas, 79x50". Cordier & Ekstrom, Inc., New York. Ill. p. 66.

*Untitled II. 1962. Oil on canvas, 79x50". Cordier & Ekstrom, Inc., New York. Ill. p. 67.

MARISOL

Born in Paris, May 22, 1930, of Venezuelan parentage (Marisol Escobar). Studied at Ecole des Beaux-Arts, Paris. To New York to live, 1950. Studied at Hans

Hofmann School and Art Students League, New York. One-man shows: Leo Castelli, New York, 1958; Stable Gallery, New York, 1962. In collections of Albright-Knox Art Gallery, Buffalo, New York; The Museum of Modern Art, New York; Rose Art Museum, Brandeis University, Waltham, Massachusetts.

*The Bathers. 1961-62. Construction of painted wood, plaster, etc. 7'x70½" (panel), 58" deep. Private collection, New York. Ill. p. 70.

*The Blacks. 1961-62. Construction of painted wood, plaster, etc., 6'6"x26". Mrs. Eleanor Ward, New York. Ill. p. 72.

*The Generals. 1961-62. Construction of painted wood, plaster, etc. 7'3"x6'4". Albright-Knox Art Gallery, Buffalo, New York. Ill. p. 73.

*Mona Lisa. 1961-62. Painted wood and plaster, 66x 11¾". Mrs. Babette Newburger, New York. Ill. p. 69.

*The Family. 1962. Construction of painted wood, plaster, etc., 6'10½"x65½". The Museum of Modern Art, New York, purchase. Ill. p. 71.

CLAES THURE OLDENBURG

Born in Stockholm, Sweden, January 28, 1929. Brought up in Chicago, where his father was consul-general for Sweden, 1936-58. Yale University, B.A. degree, 1950. Apprentice newspaper reporter, Chicago News Bureau, 1950-51. Studied at Art Institute of Chicago, 1953-54. To New York to live, 1956. One-man shows: Judson Gallery, New York, 1959; Reuben Gallery, New York, 1960; The Store (his own studio), New York, 1961; Green Gallery, New York, 1962; "Happenings," New York: Snapshots from the City, Judson Gallery, 1960; Blackouts, Reuben Gallery, 1960; Ironworks and Fotodeath, Reuben Gallery, 1961; Ray Gun Theatre (Store Days, Nekropolis, Injun, Voyages, World's Fair), The Store, 1962. Also Injun, Dallas Museum for Contemporary Arts, Texas, 1962; Gayety, University of Chicago, 1962; Stars, Washington Gallery of Modern Art, Washington, D. C., 1963. In collection of The Museum of Modern Art, New York.

*Ray Gun. 1959. Newsprint over wire frame, 39x40". Collection the artist. Ill. p. 75.

Céline, Backwards. 1959. Newsprint over wire frame, 32x40". Collection the artist.

*Red Tights. 1961. Enamel paint on plaster, 69⅝x 34¼". The Museum of Modern Art, New York, gift of G. David Thompson. Ill. p. 77.

*Shirt. 1961. Enamel paint on plaster, 48x30". Mr. and Mrs. Robert C. Scull, New York. Ill. p. 76.

*7 Up. 1961. Enamel paint on plaster, 54x36". Mr. and Mrs. Burton Tremaine, Meriden, Connecticut. Ill. p. 79.

*Strong Arm. 1961. Enamel paint on plaster, 41x32". Mr. and Mrs. Burton Tremaine, Meriden, Connecticut. Ill. p. 79.

*Sewing Machine. 1961. Enamel paint on plaster, 46½x63½". Collection the artist. Ill. p. 76.

Cash Register. 1961. Enamel paint on plaster, 27x35". Green Gallery, New York.

Green Shoes. 1962. Enamel paint on plaster, 12x16". Jon Nicholas Streep, New York.

Case of Pastries and Sundaes. 1962. Enamel paint on plaster, in glass showcase, 24x30x12". Sidney Janis, New York.

*Dual Hamburgers. 1962. Enamel paint on plaster, 7x14¾". The Museum of Modern Art, Philip C. Johnson Fund. Ill. p. 78.

AD REINHARDT

Born in Buffalo, New York, December 24, 1913. To New York, 1915. Columbia College, B.A. degree, 1935; Institute of Fine Arts, New York University, 1946-50. Worked on WPA Federal Art Project, New York, 1936-38. Member, American Abstract Artists, 1937-47. In U. S. Navy, 1945. Traveled in Europe, 1952; Asia, 1958. Teaching: Brooklyn College, since 1947; California School of Fine Arts, San Francisco, 1950; University of Wyoming, Laramie, 1951; School of Fine Arts, Yale University, 1952-53; New York University, 1955; Syracuse University, Syracuse, New York, 1957; Hunter College, New York, since 1959. Has published many articles in Art International, Art News, College Art Journal, It Is., exhibition catalogues, etc. Lives in New York. One-man shows: Artists' Gallery, New York, 1944; Brooklyn Museum Art School Gallery, 1946; Betty Parsons Gallery, New York, yearly 1946-56, 1960; Syracuse University Gallery, 1957; Stadtische Museum, Leverkusen, Germany, 1961; Iris Clert Gallery, Paris, 1961; Dwan Gallery, Los Angeles, 1962. In collections of Baltimore Museum of Art; Albright-Knox Art Gallery, Buffalo, New York; Dayton Art Institute, Dayton, Ohio; Los Angeles County Museum; University of Nebraska Art Galleries, Lincoln; Stadtische Museum, Leverkusen, Germany; Yale University Art Gallery, New Haven, Connecticut; The Museum of Modern Art, New York; Whitney Museum of American Art, New York; Oslo Museum, Oslo, Norway; Philadelphia Museum of Art; San Francisco Museum of Art; Toledo Museum of Art, Toledo, Ohio.

Abstract Painting, 1960. Oil on canvas, 60x60″. Collection the artist.

*Abstract Painting, 1960-61. Oil on canvas, 60x60″. Betty Parsons Gallery, New York. Ill. p. 84.

*Abstract Painting, 1960-61. Oil on canvas, 60x60″. The Museum of Modern Art, New York, purchase. Ill. p. 81.

Abstract Painting, No. 5, 1962. Oil on canvas, 60x60″. Iris Clert, Paris.

Abstract Painting, No. 3, 1960-63. Oil on canvas, 60x 60″. Collection the artist.

Abstract Painting, No. 4, 1963. Oil on canvas, 60x60″. Dwan Gallery, Los Angeles.

Abstract Painting, No. 6, 1963. Oil on canvas, 60x60″. Collection the artist.

JAMES ROSENQUIST

Born in Grand Forks, North Dakota, November 29, 1933. Grew up in Minnesota. Studied at University of Minnesota with Cameron Booth. Scholarship to Art Students League, New York, 1955. Worked as itinerant billboard painter and industrial painter in New York, Brooklyn, Bronx, and in Minnesota, 1953-58. Lives in New York. One-man show: Green Gallery, New York, 1962. In collection of Pasadena Art Museum, Pasadena, California.

*Pushbutton. 1960-61. Oil on canvas, 6′11″x8′9½″. Dott. Giuseppe Panza di Biumo, Milan, Italy. Ill. p. 89.

*The Light that Won't Fail, I. 1961. Oil on canvas, 6x8′. Joseph H. Hirshhorn Collection, Greenwich, Connecticut. Ill. p. 88.

*Waves. 1962. Oil on canvas, 56″x6′6″. Dott. Giuseppe Panza di Biumo, Milan, Italy. Ill. p. 90.

*Marilyn Monroe I. 1962. Oil on canvas, 7′9″x6′. Sidney Janis, New York. Ill. p. 92.

*Portrait of the Scull Family. 1962. Oil on canvas with appendage, 6′7″x7′9″. Mr. and Mrs. Robert C. Scull, New York. Ill. p. 91.

Air Hammer. 1962. Oil on canvas, 6′6½″x64½″. Dott. Giuseppe Panza di Biumo, Milan, Italy. Detail ill. p. 87.

*Over the Square. 1963. Oil on canvas, 7x7′. The Green Gallery, New York. Ill. p. 93.

JASON SELEY

Born in Newark, New Jersey, May 20, 1919. Cornell University, 1936-40. B.A. degree; two-years' study of architecture. Studied with Zadkine at Art Students League, New York, 1943-45. In Haiti, 1946-49, 1953; travel and maintenance grant for creative sculpture from U. S. Office of Education and Department of State. Fulbright fellowship to Europe, 1949-50; studied at Ecole des Beaux-Arts, Paris. Traveled in Europe again, 1961. Teaches at Hofstra University, Hempstead, New York. Lives in New York. One-man shows: Le Centre d'Art, Port-au-Prince, Haiti, 1946, 1948, 1949; American British Art Center, New York, 1947, 1948; Associated American Artists, New York, 1955; Barone Gallery, New York, 1960; Country Art Gallery, Westbury, New York, 1961; Kornblee Gallery, New York, 1962. In collections of Newark Museum, Newark, New Jersey; Chase Manhattan Bank, New York; The Museum of Modern Art, New York; St. Trinité Episcopal Cathedral, Port-au-Prince, Haiti.

Masculine Presence. 1961. Welded steel automobile bumpers, 7′3″x48″. The Museum of Modern Art, gift of Dr. and Mrs. Leonard Kornblee.

*Anjou. 1961. Welded steel automobile bumpers, 62″ high. Kornblee Gallery, New York. Ill. p. 96.

Baroque Portrait III. 1961. Welded steel automobile bumpers, 60½x45″. Kornblee Gallery, New York.

*The Anatomy Lesson. 1962. Welded steel automobile bumpers, 27x53″. Kornblee Gallery, New York. Ill. p. 98.

*Canterbury. 1962. Welded steel automobile bumpers, 46x13″. Kornblee Gallery, New York. Ill. p. 99.

*Le Roi Soleil. 1962. Welded steel automobile bumpers, 50x63″. Kornblee Gallery, New York. Ill. p. 95.

*The Boys from Avignon. 1962-63. Welded steel automobile bumpers, 58″x7′1″. Kornblee Gallery, New York. Ill. p. 97.

*Flip. 1963. Welded steel automobile bumpers, 30½x 26″. Kornblee Gallery, New York. Ill. p. 99.

DAVID SIMPSON

Born in Pasadena, California, January 20, 1928. Studied at California School of Fine Arts, San Francisco, 1949-50, 1955-56; San Francisco State College, 1957-58, M.A. degree. Teaches at Contra Costa Junior College, Concord, California. Lives in Port Richmond, California. One-man shows: San Francisco Art Association Gallery, 1958; San Francisco Museum of Art, 1959; David Cole Gallery, San Francisco, 1959; Esther-Robles Gallery, Los Angeles, 1960; Santa Barbara Museum, Santa Barbara, California, 1960; M. H. de Young Memorial Museum, San Francisco, 1961; Robert Elkon Gallery, New York, 1961, 1963; Joachim Gallery, Chicago, 1962. In collections of The Museum of Modern Art, New York; Oakland Art Museum, Oakland, California; San Francisco Museum of Art.

Tide I. 1961. Oil on canvas, 7'x49½". Joseph H. Hirshhorn Collection, Greenwich, Connecticut. Ill. p. 101.

Earthshine. 1962. Oil on canvas, 8'x43½". The Abrams Family Foundation, New York. Ill. p. 105.

Red Blue Purple. 1962. Oil on canvas, 48⅛" diameter. The Museum of Modern Art, New York, Larry Aldrich Foundation Fund. Ill. p. 103.

Orient Line. 1962. Oil on canvas, 60x37½". Professor William Rubin, New York. Ill. p. 102.

Fire Wall. 1962. Oil on canvas, 8'x37½". Robert Elkon Gallery, New York. Ill. p. 104.

Night Boundary. 1962. Oil on canvas, 8'x49½". Robert Elkon Gallery, New York.

Blue Ladder. 1962. Oil on canvas, 53½x20". David Cole Gallery, San Francisco.